A Child of War

by Helga Kelly

Helga R. Kelly

Oct. 5, 2013

Cover and book layout/design by
  Loralee L. Olson-Arcand
  Word Services Unlimited
  N9034 Lanetta Drive
  Brillion, WI 54110
  920.540.4656
  loraleeo@wordservicesunlimited.com
  www.wordservicesunlimited.com

First Printing (September 2013) by
  Seaway Printing Company, Inc.
  1609 Western Avenue
  Green Bay, WI 54303
  920.468.1500

Printed in the United States.

Dedication

This book is written in Memory of my Mom and Dad, my heroes.

To my sister Monika for encouraging me and helping with the photos.

My thanks to Karen Nuthals for typing the first edition.

To John Maino for his interest in my stories and for interviewing me.

All the photos in this book are from my Grandparents on both sides and from my brother, who saved Mom's album, not knowing how important they would be for our Family Story.

Helga with typist Karen Nuthals.

Can You Imagine?

Can you imagine…as mom and dad always started telling stories to friends and family. Can you image playing a game you could have won if the sirens wouldn't have sounded? Can you imagine when an air raid was over, you go outside and the houses that were there just the day before were all in ruins, rubble, burning or smoldering? Can you imagine a whole street gone in one afternoon? Friends or children from your neighborhood that had disappeared and you would never see them again? Can you feel the pain of just not losing a person but so many relatives in only one year? Do you think you will ever recover from shocking scenes of the horrible memories burned into your brain? Starving children, wounded people roaming the streets begging for water, a crumb of bread, or first aid, or pray with them before they die? Can you imagine how hungry you must have been to chew a piece of leather to calm your stomach? Eating dandelions for spinach? Cooking soup with only one potato and salt? Try it and you will see for yourself. Do you know how terrible nightmares can be? Death people follow you in your sleep. SS soldiers following you but you try to run away but can't run fast enough. Can you imagine a horse falling down from exhaustion and people running outside to cut meat from the horse so they could eat for a few more days? Can you imagine your mom preparing you to die when you were seven or eight years old? Stuck in a bunker with dead and wounded people never knowing if anybody will ever find you while you are still alive? Can you image being stuck in debris up to your chest and having to dig yourself out with your poor little hands bleeding and blistering from all the hard work? Can you image the pain in your ears from the pressure of an explosion that broke your eardrum? Can you imagine the sorrow when your special doll was blanketed with debris and your whole house and bed was destroyed? Can you see when your whole world gets turned around by all the destruction of a war? How brutal some people be starting wars without thinking of children anymore? Can hundreds and thousands of children ever recover and live normal lives? Will the children of this world ever have a voice? Have you ever seen the empty stare of young people coming back from the war front where they had seen too much for their minds to bear? The would never forget the roar of bombs, grenades, and gun fire. Have you ever listened to soldiers talking amongst themselves of how terrifying it was in the fox holes with rats and in the icy cold infested with lice and starving? With mangled bodies all around them? Have you heard the comrades telling how young soldiers lost their minds or defecated in their pants from being so terrified? Crazy with fear and running right into the fire because they just couldn't handle it anymore? Or talking of the deserters who fled to the mountains to hide from all the turmoil? And of the heroes who carried wounded on their backs only to find out the wounded had died before they could make it back to safety? Then turn back and go and help others? Some of those helped survived to tell about it. Or how rats ate on some of the wounded before they would die? Some soldiers can't talk of this to people who have never been there. Many people coming back from war cannot believe in God anymore because of the terror they been through. There was so much unsaid because there was no point to do so. Nothing made it easier. The soldiers in France, Flandern and Russia all had to deal with the same issues. Many stories of kindness would be told after the war. Stories of the sweat of the fear, the smell of engine oil, smoke and of the thousand yard stare as soldiers call it, when they are broken inside and their minds are wounded for life.

A Child of War

Table of Contents

A Child of War

Memories of Berlin

I was born in late April 1937, the second daughter of Ilse and Gerhardt Wartenberg. Sister Inge was only one year and one month older than me. Our parents were self-employed tailors. We lived in a four story house. Our parent's business was the whole front side of the downstairs. Big store front windows showed the goods our parents produced. They worked for the German Military as contractors making gala dress uniforms for the officers. Our mom made the fancy dresses for the officer's ladies. Our address used to be Berlin Liebig Strasse, number 147 at least until

Helga is born 1937 – April.

June 13, 1944. Our favorite place was the Berlin Zoo. We could play outside there. Pictures from that time show how happy we were and how special we were dressed. Mom and dad would let us play in the store windows where we showed off our dresses and coats our parents made for us. We pretended to be living mannequins since the real mannequins wore military uniforms. People would smile at us and even applaud us. On our old street all the parades and the noise of all the boots on the cobblestone street made me afraid. That is why we mostly stayed inside. I was afraid of noises. So it was special when mom took us away to Hoppe Garden which was the race track of Berlin or to the Zoo. We could play on the manicured lawns

My sister and I at the Berlin Zoo (Tiergarten). 1940

there. On the weekends we usually went to our grandparents' place on the waterfront of Koenigswusterhausen, a suburb of Berlin. Since the marching bands and the heavy boots on the cobblestone streets hurt my ears so bad, I was only too happy to get away from it all. We loved to play on the green lawns, in the sand, and in the water. In the big city, the houses had no front or back yards. There was only a little place in the back of the houses where people could put their garbage cans, and a little shed where people put their bicycles. Only the military and the SS used cars. Dad built a sandbox next to the storage shed. We had two more children living in that house and sometimes we all played together in the sandbox. All too often we had to run to the bunkers in the cellar of our house because of air raids. On the weekend in our grandfather's house, the whole family came together. There were dad's two sisters Editha and Gloria with their children, our cousins, Gisela and Edeltraut, and Gloria's son Joachim. Uncle Harry, a friendly, humorous guy was Aunt Gloria's husband and Joachim's father. He was Jewish and so was Uncle Heinie, Editha's husband. Grandmother Wallie Wartenberg's home was filled with laughter and music and happy faces all weekend long. Our grandfather, Erich Wartenberg, worked at the water works and was often on duty weekends. Uncle Harry was a piano player in the Rosemeir Band. He was well known in Berlin, and we liked to sing his hits. We often heard him play on the radio when we were allowed to have them. The Rosemeirs were expecting their second child and they were building a big, new house close to grandmother's waterfront. Just as the house was done the baby arrived. It was a wonderful baby girl with dark curls and big black eyes named Gloria. She was so sweet I could barely wait to see her every week. My sister and I sang all the way those 30 kilometers to grandmother's house on the street car. Many people often sang with us. Mom many times went with us to Wann Sea Beach. We liked to swim and play in the shallow water. Our grandmother followed us there but she always walked behind us because of a bad hip which made her limp. She walked behind us to hide her limp from us. But we knew she limped. We loved her more because of it. She spoiled us terribly during that time. She always had something special for us. For example she would put red sugar and a spoon of melted butter over our noodles. We couldn't explain where she bought the red sugar or the spoon of butter. That was my favorite and I couldn't get enough of it. In war time nobody had red sugar except grandma.

There was an invitation in the mail one day inviting us to the baby's baptism and the new house that the Rosemeirs had built. A rabbi was there wearing a top hat and a long black coat. He had curls down the side of his ears. We had to giggle all the time because we had never seen a man with long black curls before. The new house was very wonderful and fancy. The rooms were large and so high. I had to crane my neck way back to see the crystal chandelier. Our cousin Joe had a great big leather chair. An airplane model took up the whole corner of the room. Many friends came to see the baby and the house. A waiter served champagne and a maid served the children hot chocolate and cookies. What a day to remember! I loved the leather chair in Joe's room so much. I went to the room and fell asleep in the chair, thereby missing most of the party. Later on I went to the backyard where they had a swing set and cried

Oma Wallie's house, Koenigswusterhausen. Mom, Inge and Helga. 1939

5

1941 at Aunt Gloria's new house. First build was the swing set. Inge made me wait all the time.

every time I had to give up the swing to someone else. You could see on pictures I was crying because I was afraid of everything. I loved my sister very much but even at that young, tender age I was jealous of my sister's curly hair. It was modern at the time to wear big butterfly bows in your hair. Mine always fell off as I was walking around. My hair would not hold the heavy butterfly and that was another reason for crying.

Mom made me little hats with a big bow underneath my chin so I had a bow, a nice looking hat and was happy again. Mom always knows how to make us happy. We had very little to eat but mom found ways to make us feel full and nurtured. The most remarkable things she did on Easter and Christmas. She bought

In Grandma's backyard in Koenigswusterhausen (Berlin). 1939

almond paste and made us little apples, pear, bananas, or a little ladybug and even little pigs. She put them on plates with some candy she made out of sugar and some cookies she baked. Each of us received such a colorful plate. What a nice memory.

Dad's Store

As I mentioned before, dad's store was interesting and so much fun to discover all the things he worked with. The big store front windows made the room light and bright. The worktable that separated the storage area from the storefront reached from one wall to the other. There was a corner for some chairs and tables with catalogs on them for the newest look of dresses, skirts, uniforms and suits.

This is how Dad's store would have looked, but our building was destroyed by bombs.

Mom and Dad

On the back wall all across the room were shelves reaching from floor to ceiling. Big rolls of material were stored there. Material for summer dresses, fine silks, materials for uniforms and materials for children's clothing, like a palette of colors that always fascinated us.

On the worktable itself were big drawers, his needles, pencils, charcoal and buttons small and big were stored. Oh the buttons, now wonderful we could play. We learned counting the buttons so we could give everyone the same amount. His flatirons were stored at the end of the workbench, close to the window. Dad needed light to iron the garments. He had a whole stack of tea towels which he made wet, wound them almost dry, and put the towels on the garment in order not to make them shine when he ironed them.

Mom's ironing board was closer to the living room so she could keep an eye on us children.

When customers arrived she would come in to the family room, close the door behind her so the customers would not be disturbed. She would play with us to keep us quiet.

Dad worked in a happy way. He was always in a good mood and sang and whistled like a little bird. Often mom was singing with him and wasn't that a nice duet. He sat there on top of that workbench with his legs crossed. He would sit there for hours at a time. Mom would bring him some coffee from time to time. He really enjoyed a good cup of coffee. Three o'clock in the afternoon was the traditional coffee hour. In all Berlin people would take an hour to enjoy their coffee. My family, my sisters and brothers still keep the s a m e tradition.

Back to the store, we were allowed to play with the leftover

Berlin, Liebigstrasse 1941. In back of our house. Inge and I in outfits and hats our mom made.

fabric. We used the little rests of charcoal on our charcoal board in our room. The rest of the sowing silks. We put patches together and made dresses for our dolls but we always had to ask Dad for permission before cutting something up. Mom and dad showed us how to put materials together for our little projects. We helped to sort the yarns and put them in their drawers by color and size.

In the evening mom would sweep the parquet floor with a big broom. We girls could help her with dusting. We picked up clutter. Everything had to be tip-top as dad used to say. Ready and clean for the customer the next day. This was a time where we all still were happy, even with the interruptions from the nightly air raids.

Often in the morning the whole store had a new appearance. Mom and dad did rearrange the customer corner or put the small shelves with the brochures in another place. Happily singing we would be greeted and hugged and kissed from our parents in the morning.

We could smell when dad did some steam ironing of the heavy materials for a winter coat or suit. We were waiting for the hissing sound, zzzzzzzzzz, there it was. That is how it sounded. We never came close up to him when he needed to steam, it was too dangerous. We could get burned by the steam.

Dad used a tea towel to steam garments so there would not be a shine left behind. He had tons of them on the shelf on the worktable. He had to make them wet just a little so he would not damage the garment. There are so many things I still do the same way as he showed us. It is amazing what you learn as a child and do automatically the same way later in life.

One day a man came in to the store, was shy to start speaking until we were hushed out of the room. After he left we had a wonderful red Persian carpet on our floor. It was very large and filled the whole store front of the room. Just what we needed to make the store more elegant. So much fun for all of us, sitting on the rug and having tea time, playing with our dolls and later on having our little baby brother sleeping on it. Bargaining, said dad. He could not pay his bill, did not want to owe us anything and gave us the rug for dad's work. What a noble payment. In war time you have to be flexible, help people as they help you, dad told us.

Our dad had three sewing machines in the shop. He had a large tailor table which extended from wall-to-wall in his shop for cutting material and pressing and for hand sewing. There were shelves on each side of the table for storing materials and tools of the trade. There were tables and chairs for the customers in the shop. He always whistled or sang when at work. There were mannequins in the two big windows and when dad babysat us we played in those windows. The mannequins were our kings, queens and princesses. When we played the store window was our castle. Many people watched as we were dressed in the finest horticulture and that was in the middle of the war. Dad had good talent for dressing us and his officers. He was lucky to be at home because the military needed him still.

It was Christmas 1942 and the bombs were falling every night but during the day time people got ready for Christmas. A few streets down from us on Wasau Boulevard was the Christmas market. There were booths where they sold Christmas ornaments and German bakery. Toys and candles were sold, too. There was a sweet, heavy smell

Two loving sisters in the park. 1939

in the air of cinnamon and apple cider. On every corner there were booths with Christmas candies. People with smiling faces were buzzing around from booth to booth. The war was forgotten for a few hours.

Mom made coffee for dad after the walk to the Christmas Park and we all sat around the fireplace. Our little brother, Gerhard Jr, was about four months old. It would be his first Christmas. He was a cute little bundle of joy and often made us laugh. Mom was still thin and sick from giving birth. We all got very thin and dad had to wear a belt. It was necessary to adjust the belt from time to time a notch down.

One day mom took us to the milk store located on Melmer Street, which was very special. There was a farm in the middle of the big city. Only milk products were sold there. The milk had to be stirred by the salesman with a big wooden paddle because the cream had not been separated. The salesman explained that products that hadn't been sold in the milk store were loaded on a train which passed behind the store and was to be taken to the war front. Tanks, trucks cattle, wood and coal were shipped there also.

Work came in slowly for dad now because Hitler needed the officers at the war theater. Even dad

Traditional Tile Stove with seating bench.

was drafted and received orders to go to France. He was forced to join the Hitler Party after he was drafted.

It was only a little walk to get to the Alexander Platz with its big shopping centers. Herti was dad and mom's favorite store. That is where they bought all the materials for the tailor shop. The store owner was Jewish. His name was Herman Tiez. Hitler's party shortened the store name to Herti so it wouldn't sound so Jewish. Herti is still the name of the store today. There was another very special street called "Under the Linden" where there were benches under the big, old Linden trees. People held hands while strolling under the linden trees. It was called lovers lane. All those wonderful memories are still in my memory because of the help of my mom and dad and from listening to the stories told around the fireplace. There were no TV's at that time. Most of the radios were confiscated so we couldn't hear the negative news. But bad news travels on foot too.

Whenever I think about those times I recall the visits to the milk store. Cheeses were displayed in a display case. I even remember the smell. I still see the wooden paddles in my mind and the milk cans with handles on either side. I had never seen a cow before and was scared at first. But after a while I even petted the little pink nose of a newborn calf. I still remember the whole layout of the store after a whole lifetime. All of the pleasant memories are still in my mind. I remember the impressive buildings in the city, especially the Brandenburger gate which was the door to the city. It was a monument that had the gate of the Kaiser astride a horse on its top. A second monument was on the Kurfuersten Damm, which had a mounted king on it's top. (Kaiser Franz Josef)

Childhood Memories of Berlin 1937=1944

Sirens blared from every direction. The noise was sounding painfully in my head. Even pressing my hands over my ears didn't help. Sorry my child, my mom said, we have to be warned. Airplanes are on their way already. We must rush to the bunkers to avoid the bombs. I complained, I don't want to go to that place again. We were aroused from our sleep twice last night and I am so tired. Be patient my child, said mom. This is war. Maybe we will have a snack before we go down. After checking for food she said, oh no, we can only have two meals today. We have to skip lunch. Maybe we have some crackers in the bunker. Everyone had a designated spot in the bunker where they had a cot, blankets and a gas mask. There were standard items in the bunkers. There were shelves for emergency food, clothing, flashlights and water. We were fortunate to have our bunker directly underneath our store. Mom said we even have a treat for you down there. Mom grabbed a satchel which contained our documents in one hand and my sister and I by the other hand. Taking the satchel to the bunker was

Brandenburger Tor

Friedrich der Große

Checkpoint Charlie

Berlin's Monuments and important Landmarks, Tiergarten – Zoo

compulsory. We dashed out of our flat, pushing and shoving for the bunker where we settled into our designated place. Then we sat and waited. Zoom. The airplanes came. Sometimes they flew so low that the houses shook. We children were thrown off our bunks by the thundering explosions of the bombs. My ears, my ears, I cried. It hurts and I can't stand it. It is driving me wild. I know, dear mom comforted me. The planes will soon be gone and we can relax. Come on, I will read you a story. My sister endured all of these explosive sessions without a murmur. She kept right on playing with her paper dolls and was unaware about the terrible turmoil about her. She didn't even wear her ear plugs. Eventually the shrill monitor alarm sounded which released us from the bunkers. While all this terrible bombing took many lives, to me it was meaningless. As far as I was concerned it was just an interruption to our normal daily existence. On the Christmas before, the SS

Leftovers of the Wall

picked up Uncle Heinie at work. They didn't even notify Editha, his wife. A co-worker of Uncle Heinie came and brought the terrible news. He told Aunt Editha that four men had come and picked him up at his work bench. No one had a telephone in those days. Only the elite group from Hitler and the upper crust had them. About ten days later our poor aunt received a letter in the mail from the German General Staff Headquarters. There was a death certificate in the letter which said that her husband had died of pneumonia. Pneumonia always appeared on Jewish death certificates. It was recommended in the same letter that she assume her maiden name of Wartenberg. It was further recommended that her children take the name of Wartenberg so they wouldn't be expelled from school. That was a sad Christmas. We celebrated the life of Uncle Heinie just as we had done with Uncle Harry. We placed a cross in grandma's backyard. There weren't any churches or synagogues anymore. So we just prayed at home. Since our dad had to go to war, Editha and her two girls moved in with us. That was fun for us children. All of these events came at Christmas. There still wasn't any word from or about cousin Joe. We children asked dad if he could look for Joe when he went to France. Aunt Gloria couldn't get over the loss of Uncle Harry and took sick. She became deeply depressed because she saw no way out. Grandmother Wally made her move in with her so she could care for her and the baby. Mom, dad and Editha and all five children went to grandmother's house so they all could say good-bye to dad's parents. This time there was no singing or laughing because we were all so sad. Grandmother had not seen our little brother for a while and in the meantime he was walking and talking. Everyone that was left of our sweet family was there. We spent a good week with grandma and grandpa and we all felt better. Suddenly little baby Gloria took violently sick. They had to feed her milk which was spoiled and the little baby threw up everything that she ate. She developed a high fever and diarrhea. Little Gloria didn't make it through the night. I was lying in my bed and was awakened by a terrible scream. I was still dizzy from sleep as I walked down to mom but she was not there. So I went towards the light that came out of baby Gloria's room. The grown-ups didn't even notice me at first. Everybody was crying. I

Koenigswusterhausen at Grandma Wallie's waterfront home. Mom, Tante Gloria, Joachim, Inge, Helga and Cousin Edeltraut. 1943

went to the baby's bed and my heart pounded a thousand miles an hour. What was wrong with our sweet baby Gloria? Her eyes were wide open but she stared into space without moving. I touched her tiny hand. She usually smiled when she was touched but nothing happened now. I got real scared and pulled mom's arm. She just pulled me into her arms, and I noticed she was shaking. "Mom, what happened," I asked? Mom said, "Gloria is a little angel now." Grandma called the neighbor and sent him for a doctor. When he came he gave Aunt Gloria a shot. Aunt Gloria could not stop screaming. She needed help. For the baby, all help came too late. The doctor said Aunt Gloria had a nervous breakdown so he sent for an

Mom expecting Baby Gerhard. 1940

ambulance. In a little while four men in white came and put Aunt Gloria in a strait jacket. They crossed her arms in front of her and tied them to the back. She screamed even more and jumped up and down. Then she rolled on the floor. The four men grabbed her by the arms and legs, then carried her outside. We called to her and said we will come and see you. She probably didn't even hear us. After burying little Gloria in grandma's backyard, we had to go home and to school. Our dad had to go to the battle field. He didn't know at that time that he was not to see his younger sister again. And Gloria's nerves were totally shot from all the pain she had to endure. She had lost two children and a husband in such a short time. The next terrible thing was just waiting to happen. Having a Jewish name and being at a nerve clinic was the worst that could happen to her. She fell under the law of euthanasia. Medicine was too hard to come by and the doctors were forbidden to give medicine to Jewish people.

It was considered a waste of medicine. It could help a soldier in the field. She never left the hospital alive and we never saw her again. After a

Gerhard is born; here with Inge. Berlin 1940

few weeks, grandma received Gloria's ashes, and they were buried in little Gloria's grave. It was noted on her death certificate that she died from pneumonia. A whole family wiped off the face of the earth in a short time of less than a year. Mr. Hitler, we wish you the same terrible fate. We didn't have

Mom with Inge and Gerhard. 1941

much time to grieve. The air raids came more often, in shorter intervals with more force. Airplanes bombed whole sections of Berlin. We couldn't go to school. At first only industrial areas were bombed but later on almost every house that was intact was destroyed. We spent much more time in our bunker than in our living quarters. Mom had a hard time getting all of us down to the bunkers safely. It was hard running down the staircase with three children every time. People were horrified and afraid so they pushed and scrambled. It didn't matter to them if there were children. They all wanted to be safe first. We children screamed when we had to put the gas masks on but it was mandatory. We had to do it or we would be forced to leave the bunker. The house we lived in was a four story giant and there were sixteen families living in it. With the sound of sirens almost 40 people would run down the stairway at the same time. No one would be polite and die as a hero. Everyone wanted to survive. We had field cots, clothing and food down there. It wasn't worthwhile running upstairs for cooking anymore. There was a camper stove and an electric oven in the bunker now and lots and lots of water. We had to stock up on food, blankets, clothing and pillows. Everything needed for life. Thank God we prepared because we would need it later. Our mom had stored toys in the bunker. She had thought of everything to keep us occupied. Dad rang the bell suddenly one morning and surprised us with a visit. He was wounded and was on leave. Mom said later that God had sent him to rescue his whole family. He and some of his friends were building something in the store. I wondered what they were doing. It sounded like they were breaking the whole house down because it was so noisy. They finished up after a hard week of labor. Dad introduced us to a wonderful slide they had built that was to be used to slide to our part of the bunker. What a helpful thing. How nice it was to see that he was concerned about us. We had to use this slide many, many times. Later on I heard dad telling mom how bad it was at the war front. There was no gasoline, ammunition or boots for their feet. Dad told mom that he had heard at the war front that German soldiers were dying from starvation and freezing to death in Russia. Dad thought things weren't going right and wished the fighting was over with. But Hitler needed more soldiers and he did the unthinkable. He sent old men to France, Italy, and Holland. He drafted thousands and thousands of young boys ages 15 to 18 years old. They were trained for a very short time then sent to the home front. World War II was not over yet. All bridges were guarded by teenagers and a few old men that were too old for the battle field. Hitler hid in his safe hideout in his bunker in Berlin. The SS had their hands full to find the last Jews in Germany.

Thousands of POWs died in the stockades. Was there any hope for us? Our grandpa Erick Wartenberg came to see us in Berlin because mail didn't work too good anymore. He came to check on us. He was the one to use the slide for the first time. He made us laugh because he pretended to be scared at first. On this visit he told us that the British had bombed the water works where he worked. He would be out of work until repairs were made. He told us that grandma was okay but she missed us terribly. We could not risk traveling by street car anymore, those 30 kilometers because there were air raids over the city by this time, night and day. People were afraid to leave their houses. It was good to see grandpa. We enjoyed the day with him. He was a good storyteller and time went fast until it was time to go home. On June 13, 1944, it happened that we sat in our basement and listened to the noise of the coming bombers. We were shaking from fear again and wished it was over with. The bombs sounded louder and closer and there were flying so low that the walls were shaking from the heavy sounds. Plaster crumpled and fell to the floor making so much dust that it was hard to breathe. That was the sign for us to put our gas masks on. Suddenly there was an enormous explosion. My ears seam to burst and the house was really shaking. But it was not our house that had been bombed. It was a house across the street. We were grateful to see we were okay for another time when we got out. We had a person living in our house, Mr. Himmler. He was responsible that the people living in our house went to the bunker during an air raid. He called himself the overseer and we had to call him the ortsfuehrer. He told us that he was a close relative of Himmler, one of Hitler's best friends. He had to make sure that all doors in the flat were locked so nothing could be stolen. He wore the party uniform but walked with a limp and was not able to be drafted. Sometimes people smiled behind his back and said, yeah and I am Hitler's little brother. They just let him talk and thought he was a show off. Our two cousins, the two children from the third floor, and the three of us were the only children in the big house. The other occupants, for the most part, were elderly. We all got along very well, and they read to us and played puppets with us when we sat for hours in the bunker. The grown-ups played cards while the elderly ladies knitted. One old gentleman made baskets. He made one for my dog, a stuffed animal. I thought he was the nicest one of them all, very quiet but friendly. The other people were nice too but when I or my little brother cried or screamed because he was hungry they raised their eyebrows as a sign of disapproval. You could have children at this time but they weren't allowed to be heard. So at that time we read a book, painted with water colors or tried to be invisible. Often when a bomb fell on a neighbor's house, the enormous pressure lifted us off the chairs or beds. But the worst part was that it was so difficult to breathe because the pressures acted like a vice on your chest. When we could breathe again the panic was over and there was no reason to cry anymore. After a while we were so used to this terror that we didn't cry. We celebrated my seventh birthday in the bunker. We had candles and garlands hanging from the walls. Mom made tea and one of the other nice ladies had baked cookies. It was actually a nice party. All the people sang happy birthday to me. There was no music because everyone had to give up their radios. Some people had hidden radios but that was very dangerous. You could be thrown in jail if caught with them. People were not allowed to listen to the news but now and then we could catch a word from Mr. Himmler's radio, the only one who was allowed to have one.

We were short of milk for the baby so some of the people in the bunker gave mom their ration of powdered milk. It tasted different and at first the little boy didn't like it. But hunger made him drink it after a while. We only had three slices of bread for six people. We had to share, and we learned to share quite often every bite we ate. There was no word from dad, no wonder, in that chaos. With all this going on, Aunt Editha found a new friend. He invited her to the officer's club. They also went to a little pub now and then. She heard all kinds of news there. She told mom that the Americans were coming and they would be here soon. Hopefully we would still be alive by then. There was a big black and white event coming up at the officer's club. Our poor Aunt Editha had no dress. She asked everyone if they had any piece of material left over from their own clothes. Most people had sold everything on the black market to put food on their own tables. Everything was gone from the crystal to their feather beds. Mom had just sold her jewelry last week for a hundred pounds of potatoes and some sauerkraut. We would have something for a while. Mom found a fancy table cloth in a drawer. It was white with great big red flowers. Both ladies sat down and sewed an evening dress. One shoulder was totally bare because they ran out of material. Editha looked very nice when she tried it on. She wore a wide black belt around her waist, long black gloves and black high heels. As you would say, she was a good looking woman. Now that she had a boyfriend she decided to take her children and move into her own home. When she attended that gala party she took her children back to mom for her to babysit. It was about 10:00 p.m. when the sirens sounded, warning us of an air raid. All of us went down the slide to the bunker. Great Britain had a new weapon. The bombs were filled with phosphorus. They exploded above the surface and pieces came down like black rain. They made bombs to do as much damage to Berlin as possible. We were on their list as a target today. The pounding and explosions were never ending. It seemed they wanted to destroy the rest of Berlin that night. Our bunker filled with smoke and dust so we had to wear the gas masks again. All of a sudden we heard terrible scrams outside the door of our bunker. We heard fists pounding on the metal frame of the door. We always had to be prepared to allow other people seeking protection to enter the bunker. They sought food, water and first aid. Mr. Himmler opened the door and a person covered completely with hot phosphorus stumbled in. Our mom took a blanket and covered the person to kill the smoldering patches of phosphorous. The person was badly burned over the whole body and face. That is why we didn't know at first that this person was our Aunt Editha. She needed a doctor fast as we could not help her here. She cried and screamed and whimpered with pain while her whole body shook. The pain must have been terrible, poor Aunty. Himmler called a doctor immediately. The ambulance must have been close by because they were there in a hurry. The paramedics gave her a shot and the shaking stopped. My cousins were in tears. They had lost so much family already and they were afraid they would lose their mom too. One of the paramedics told mom the name of the hospital Aunt Editha would be taken to. But the terrible night had just begun. The sirens were howling again but the bombers were over us already. The tremor lifted us off our feet. The explosions were so loud that one of my ear drums burst and I thought I would never hear again. Concrete and dust came from the walls and blinded us. Mom had to put the gas masks over our faces. Inge, my sister and my cousins had learned to put them on their selves. Then, another explosion. The light went out. We knew we had taken a full hit. The back wall caved in and fell on the people sitting there. Screams, groans and total darkness. We heard our little brother cry. Thank God he was still alive. Mom found him with a brick on his chest and she pulled him closer to her.

We had been trained to go no further than an arm's length away from her. We were sitting directly under our slide. That saved us from injury. Other people were not so lucky. All of our possessions were under the slide. Mom found a candle and lit it. Mr. Himmler yelled at her to put it out. If there was a gas leak, we all would go up in smoke. Mom blew the candle out and found her flashlight which she turned on. A few men in the bunker tried to open the entrance door but it would not budge. Next they tried to open a trap door which led to our store. It wouldn't budge either. The other back wall caved in now, rocks and dust fell on us again. Mr. Himmler found his emergency radio but it was crushed and would not work anymore. He had a big flashlight and a shovel. They had to dig some people out. Then Mr. Himmler announced we had to make a head count. We had to check to see how many people we had lost. I couldn't stop crying because the dirt got into my eyes. My body was stuck up to my chest in mortar. I had to dig myself out with my little hands until they bled. My sister too. We needed water but there was dust and dirt in each bucket of water. Mom said it was still good to drink. She explained that our soldiers had to drink like this. Mr. Himmler and some other men read names from a list he had taken from his shirt pocket. By the count we were missing sixteen people. And another ten were injured. We needed to get out of here. People needed a doctor. Mom said she could smell death. I was so afraid of what would happen to us because Mr. Himmler told us it was possible no one would pull us out. They would need heavy equipment and there was no gasoline available. He also told us that the government had stopped digging in ruins to look for survivors. Everyone had to help themselves as much as possible. We could not move. Everything was caved in. We had no toilets anymore and I had to go. Mom emptied the water from one bucket to another leaving a small amount of water in the pail. Mom told us this was to be our toilet now. We will shut off the flashlight while you use the toilet to preserve your dignity. Then we all prayed together. Some prayed quietly and some quite loud and fearful. We were prepared if we were to be buried for good. I did not want to die. My sister and cousins either. We cried and prayed. We prayed and cried. We fell asleep eventually. We did not know if it was night or day. The smell of dead people made us sick. The old ladies started singing to keep the rats away. Mom found some crackers and gave us each one. Mom seemed to know how to handle each situation. We loved her so much and told her so. She would tell us stories in this situation to pass the time away. We heard an old man's voice begging us to help him. His leg was crushed under a beam. He could not get out and I'll bet it hurt him real bad. There was no one able to help him. Everyone was stuck one way or another. We were so helpless and alone. Some people used bad language until the shock was gone. Everyone reacted differently. We don't know how long we were under the rubble below the house. Then we heard some motors above us and some voices. They were trying to get us out. Thank God they had come to help us. Mom hammered against the wooden side with a broom stick. We screamed and yelled because who wants to die at the tender age of seven or eight? We saw a little daylight through a hole but the light was hurting our eyes. We had to close our eyes again and again until we got used to the bright sun light. It took them hours to finally get us out. Mr. Himmler asked the operator of the heavy equipment who had sent him, why our house? Why not the house on the other side of the street? The operator replied that your cousin asked us to get you out. So we said thank you to Mr. Himmler. At least you did something right in this war. We all had to go to a hospital to have a checkup. Just by chance that was the same hospital that Aunt Editha had been taken to. When we were released by the doctor we went directly to the burn unit. Aunt Editha had her whole head and face bandaged and told us that the pain was bearable now. She was glad that she is still alive and we were too. Our aunt asked mom if she would take our cousins to grandmother Wally's home and mom was only too happy to oblige so they would be in a safer haven. We went to the Red Cross after that to let them know we were still alive. The Red Cross maintained a survivor's list. At the Red Cross there was food, a bottle of milk and a bed for the night. We were taken to a large room full of beds. All the people there had experienced the same as we did. Their houses had been destroyed and they had no place to stay for the night. There was a good breakfast the next morning. A man from the Red Cross gave mom some money for a taxi. He had also given mom some train tickets to get away from the danger zone. We were to go to our mom's home town, Schleiz, located in the east part of Germany. But first we had to say goodbye to grandma Wally and grandpa Eric in Koenigswusterhausen. It took only an hour to go there in the taxi cab. The only thing we had left was on our bodies. Thank God we had received a change of clothing from the Red Cross.

Some of our belongings were at grandmother's house and mom could wear some of Aunt Gloria's clothes. Grandfather was allowed to take some personal stuff out of Gloria's house before it was confiscated. We spent a good week with our grandparents and our two cousins. It was the last time we were to see those two girls because we were separated by the wall in Berlin.

The Schramm Family

One morning while we were still at grandmas, we saw the family Schramm packing in a hurry and running to their yacht with heavy boxes. We thought they were going on a trip. The boat's name was Ruth. It was Mrs. Schramm's name too. When Ruth saw mom with us children she called to us to come over and said she had presents for the children. We went over and waited at the entrance steps. Ruth came out with her little baby David Rudi Jr. in her arms and a basket filled with presents. She smiled at us and let us hug the baby. Mom told Ruth that we had been bombed out of our house and business and had lost everything. Ruth told mom that she, her husband and baby would try to get away because they had received an order to show up with one suitcase at the military headquarters. Mom knew what that meant. While we were still visiting a military truck came up the driveway. Mom yelled to the driver that this was not a street and they couldn't just drive through people's property. The driver didn't listen to our mom. The truck stopped and ten black dressed SS soldiers jumped from the back of the truck. Their black boots made the exact noise that I hated so

Helga with new dress for 1st Grade in Koenigswusterhausen visiting Grandma Wallie. Age 6, 1943

Inge with matching dress for 2nd Grade. Age 7, 1943

much, click – click – click. They went up the stairs of the mansion where we still stood at the top of the stairs. We did not talk anymore. We just stood there frozen. We knew that this wasn't good. The soldiers started yelling, where is that Jewish pig? The SS soldiers pushed mom, Inge, our cousins, and me aside. The soldiers wanted to enter the entrance to the foyer. When Mrs. Schramm started screaming, the baby started screaming too. We just stood there in fear and were unable to move. The commotion brought Mr. Schramm out of the kitchen. He still had a kitchen knife in his hand because he had been preparing lunch. He held parsley in one hand and the knife in the other. He stood in shock when he saw the SS men. One SS man took Ruth by the arm and pulled her away. She was yanked so hard that the baby fell to the stone floor. Mom picked up the little guy and checked him for injuries as she tried to calm him. Another SS soldier started screaming, that Jewish swine has a knife in his hand. Suddenly there was a loud bang, a shot. A red spot appeared on the forehead of Mr. Schramm, not bigger than a quarter, as he fell backward to the floor. A large puddle of blood formed around his head. The shot had ripped a part of the back of his head off and he was dead before he hit the floor. The walls, floors, doors and everything was splattered with blood. Mrs. Schramm threw herself over her husband's body to cover him. All of this

Helga and Inge in front of Schramm family mansion. 1941

Cousin Joachim, age 14, Inge, Gerhard and Helga. This is the last picture of our cousin. We never heard what happened to him.

happened in seconds. Mrs. Schramm cried and her eyes were blinded by tears. The little boy in mom's arms cried, too. The murderer's wrenched Mrs. Schramm from her husband's body and pushed her brutally into the truck. They placed Mr. Schramm's body in a body bag which was just a potato sack. They threw the body bag into the truck at Ruth's feet. The soldiers locked up the mansion, put a red seal on the door, and went to the truck. Then they took the baby from mom's arms and threw him into the truck at Ruth's feet, too. We all cried and mom turned to Ruth and said, "I am ashamed to be a German." They drove off but we didn't know where to. Mom was talking to grandma and I heard her saying they will probably end up in Buchenwald or Dachau or even Auschwitz. I did not know what that meant at the time. The Schramms were good friends of mom, dad and Walli Oma. Our dad was their tailor, their friendship reached back many years. I could not sleep not knowing what those words meant. People had whispered those names before but I just didn't know what those words meant. Mom thought there was no reason to not tell me. I slept very close to her that night in her bed. Both of us wept that night and held on to each other. We had seen so much and heard so much in our young lives already. It was just one more reason to hate war more. Mom also told me that Aunt Editha did not order ration cards anymore for the two girls. Our aunt was afraid that the Nazi's would find out that the girls were half Jewish. Grandma Wallie was having the two girls until Editha was released from the hospital. Mom, Inge, me and brother Gerhard went to mom's parents in Saxonia by train with tickets from the Red Cross. On the way there we were missing our grandma, grandpa and cousins already. We only knew mom's parents, our other grandparents, from letters. There was an aunt, an uncle, and other relatives by these grandparents too. Mom came from a large family of three girls and three boys. They all lived close by. During the railroad trip many people talked by whispering. Panic showed on all of their faces. I heard for the second time that the Americans would be here soon. We also heard that women were often raped. Inge said she would kick them you know where. Sure you would, said mom. I felt stronger already. For the rest of the way we slept and prayed, except when we left the train for air raids. We finally arrived at our destination. Before we left Berlin, mom received a letter from the military saying dad had orders to go to Russia. Then the next letter said he was missing in action. Mom knew he would come back and we children had no doubts either. We had to be careful of what we were saying because no one was allowed to criticize the fuehrer. Trucks had speakers on their tops with a message from Hitler saying that he had the war in his grip and we were going by giant strides towards winning the war. How could one say we were winning when there were no houses standing and people had nothing to eat? The worst part was, there was no bread. The prayer saying "give us our daily bread" was said many times a day with lots of hope and an empty, rumbling stomach. There were times I dreamed of all the good things we had to eat before the air raids came so often. Especially about the days when mom made the little apples, bananas and oranges out of almond paste. It was funny because I had not seen a banana before my 12th birthday. I was not interested in who would win the war, I just wanted something to eat, just something to fill my stomach. I'll bet many people and children had the same desire. But the store shelves were empty. It was a wonder that children grew because everyone was thin and bony. I found out years later that senior citizens were terrified to go to a hospital for in-house treatment. Towards the end of the war they held back from going to a hospital because of the food shortage. They feared they would be next to disappear because they were no good anymore and were costing the state money. It was money that could be used in better ways. There were slogans which said, *"Feed the young, not the old. Feed the future."* We did not know then that they would eliminate old folks. The SS were openly talking about over-population and we heard later that they made many old people go to sleep forever. Often we heard Hitler speaking and screaming over the loud speakers. He always said "this is Berlin headquarters, Hitler, your fuehrer speaking. Don't give up. We will win this war. We are on the march in Russia. The whole front line gives us good reports. We will put more power on some weak spots and make them stronger. No one will get us down. We will fight to the last man. The win will be ours. Paradise waits for all of us. Don't be discouraged, believe in me and in our stronghold, the German army."

Everyone was afraid to criticize Hitler, the party or the SS. You were either for Hitler or against him. Your life was very short if you were against him. People were killed every day because they wouldn't sign for the Nazi party. If your name was not in the register for the Nazi party you could not get any ration cards. Many people went underground and ate out of garbage cans and the waste of party people. In the event of an invasion, Berlin was to be destroyed and all of the underground tunnels were to be flooded. Rumors said all of the children of Berlin, some 100,000 at the time, were to be destroyed first. The SS would come and give the parents some cyanide, a quick painless killer. How terrible whenever a boy turned fourteen years old, they would put him in training to save the home front. You could see deserters hanging from lamp posts in the mornings. The SS would destroy underground tunnels to make it more difficult to get into Berlin. All of the people living in the underground tunnels would die when the tunnels were destroyed and flooded. The SS said it would be better to die that way than to fall into the hands of the Americans or Russians. Later on the electricity, water and gas was cut off to the damaged parts of Berlin. I still wonder how many people were in the ruins. Many people living in the ruins made fire to keep warm, drank water from rivers and lakes, took sick, spread typhus and many died. On May 1, 1945, it was known Hitler had killed himself. Germany was in turmoil.

A Child of War

After the Bombing

We met Oma and Opa from Schleiz, our Aunt Hilde and our cousin Christa at the train station. We had never seen any of them before. Grandma's (Oma) smiling face made me feel comfortable from the first moment on. Grandpa (Opa) had no hair but had the bluest eyes ever. So his smiles made up for his bald head. Aunt Hilde looked really respectable but Christa was a little snob. She was a teenager already and we were only small children in her eyes. Sister Inge was eight years old and I was seven, Gerhard was only four. In a big city like Berlin we had grown up a lot faster than any teenager in a little sleepy town. We found this out after we had a chance to know each other better. As we arrived in our new home by our grandparents we were taken with everything that was there. Chicken, ducks, geese, rabbits, goats, pigs, sheep, two kittens and a dog called Snuffi. The cats were named Milli and Mini. The pig's name was name Sahra, with ten babies. The goats Lisa and Lore, the sheep was Hanna. There were apple trees full of fruit, berries on bushes, and trees with pears hanging heavy with fruit. Grandpa had honey bees, too. There was sweet corn back in the

Mom getting a perm from her cousin Christa at Aunt Hildegard's salon, 1944; after our house was bombed, we are in Schliez, our Grandma's hometown.

field and potatoes in the back yard. A vegetable garden with carrots, cabbage, snow peas, whatever you could wish for, was right there. We had landed in paradise! Behind the house we found cages with rabbits and a chicken coop. A big barn for hey and straw housed the other animals. It was just amazing. We had never met any people with so many living creatures at their farm. The stalls and barns. Mom had talked to us about her parents farm but we just could not imagine. We loved it when we met all these creatures. Then the house, it was a wonder by itself. A two-story farmhouse with lots of property. It had two complete apartments with old fashioned fire places called kacheloefen. A bathtub with claw feet sat in the middle of the white and black tiled bathroom. The bathroom had a toilet complete with a bidet. Grandpa had remodeled the upstairs bathroom but it had no tub, only a shower. Grandma had a summer kitchen in the basement. There was a little root cellar and a laundry and a big great room with chairs and couches and coffee tables, the hutches were full of china and silver. Our grandparents had six children. Mom was the youngest. There were three boys and three girls in the family. Mom's nickname was Ilsekind, sort of the same as calling her Ilse, her name and hanging on kind which meant little one. Mom was very special to her parents and we all could feel that special bond between them. Their great love

A kacheloefen

Mom in grandma's garden. 1944

Back from left to right: Opa (grandpa) Emil, Tante Erna (aunt), Tante Hildegard, Oma (grandma) Milda. Front: Cousins Verena and Christa. 1940

surrounded us all. Grandpa said to me you are just a picture of our Ilse when she was a little girl and Grandma can see in you her little daughter again. My older sister Inge was grandpa's shadow. She followed him all around the place, everywhere he went. What closeness and warmth and healing we had with this family unit. It was a healing place where we could forget the war and the hunger and living in peace, tranquility and in plenty.

By this time it was close to Christmas and we prepared for the holidays. Grandma showed us how to knit little things for mom and our aunts. Grandpa was working on the Christmas decorations also.

Nordstrasse 14, in Schleiz/Thueringen. Oma and Opa Kanz's house.

Mom had still not heard from dad since the day he arrived in Rostock. She was nervous and heavy-hearted. Every morning we saw her going to the mailbox by the fence and coming back empty-handed. We could tell by her face that there was no word from him. Mom had written letters to friends and relatives to see if they had heard from him or seen him because he would check in Berlin first. Dad did not know that we had to move to Schleiz because our house was no more. She told everyone to give him our address so that he could find us and know that we were all still alive.

The radios announced that the war was getting worse every day but we in Grandpa's house did not notice any changes in our little city. Grandpa also had his radio openly playing. In Berlin we had to give them all to the SS Nazis. It was 1944, two days before Christmas when all of a sudden there stood dad at the door. Of course, I did not even recognize him in his uniform, boots steel helmet and his gun over his shoulder. He seemed a total stranger. He did not even smell the way he used to and I remembered the way he smelled. But when mom's face lit up bright as the sun we knew suddenly that it was dad. We all drew close and he kissed us again and again. "Thank God you are all okay", he said. Then we told him that our house had been bombed, totally demolished and we were stuck underneath the ruins for three long days and nights before they were able to rescue us. We had not been able to save anything other than our papers which were in a little bag that mom sat on. We told him how we were digging with our little hands until they were bleeding, the dust was so thick it was hard to breath and our eyes were itchy and red. We told him Mr. Himmler was the alarm post in our house and that we never believed he was a relative of big Himmler, Hitler's left hand. They gave our house a complete search because Himmler's relative lived there. We told him how horribly frightened we were when the walls came crashing down. The old people form the second floor and Mrs. Mimme from the fourth floor got buried in the ruins. The entire family that lived on the fourth floor, which had the two boys, were gone. We related to him how shocked we were when his sister, Aunt Editha came burning into the bunker and that she is alive. We saw her in the hospital burn unit. We also told him about the frightening train ride with numerous interruptions because of alarms and air raids as we were en route to Schleiz, 250 miles north from Berlin, our safe haven. Mom let us talk and dad listened in silence. But he asked about his sister's daughters and his own parents. Then sadly we had to tell him about Aunt Gloria, his second sister, his niece Gloria and the Schramm family, his friends. Dad had tears in his eyes and we all cried together, washing away these bad memories. We had to tell him how the SS Nazis shot his friend in front of our eyes and how he died, all the blood around him. We hugged dad and grandpa said we were all safe and alive so let's celebrate your homecoming Gerhard. Finely we are all together! But dad said he is only on leave until January 30, 1945. He has orders to go to Rostock, in far north of Germany and from there to Russia. Momma hoped the war would be over by then and dad could stay with us instead of returning to the war. Dad had a gunshot wound in his leg from the battlefield and as soon as it would be properly healed he needed to return to war. After he went back he had to drive one of the tanks awaiting him in Rostock to Russia.

January 30th arrived much too soon and dad had to leave for about a whole year. After that we had no news from dad, only the one letter that he had reached Rostock. After dad left mom found out that she was pregnant. She wept openly as she told grandma the news. But grandma comforted her by the thought that this was a woman's duty, to bear children. She must be happy with the expectation of a new life instead of being sad and unhappy. But mom was afraid of being alone with four children. Our grandparent's assured her that they were here to help and care in every way they could. This cheered up our mom.

They really showed her how much they cared about the new baby. Grandpa went to the black market, a market where you still could buy anything for half a pig or other meat. He got her a beautiful wicker baby carriage. Mom sewed happily little white pillows from parachute silk found in the cornfield behind the house. Booties, jackets and little gloves for the new baby. On October 17, 1945, our little sister Evelyn was born. We called her Evie. She smiled a lot and was such a good sweet baby. We loved her instantly. She slept through the nights and very seldom cried. We remember that when she cried her bottom lip would look very funny. She made little corners like the lips of a carp. Grandpa was in seventh heaven. He walked up and down the street like a proud father would do. Both grandparents went plumb wild about little Evie, taking her new wicker carriage everywhere and acting like a young couple with their first child. We older sisters had a hard time to get a turn.

Our biggest disappointment was that there was no news from dad. He was gone for months but not even a shred of news came to us about him. We wondered what happened to him and why he could not write to us. We did not even know if he made it to his destination in Moscow.

In the meantime at our grandparents home, we were well fed and cared for. We showed signs of getting some meat on our bones. We began to look like the normal children of our age group instead of skeletons.

We heard on the radio that the US Army was closing in on Berlin but they had told us that months ago and we did not pay attention to that rumor. We also heard that the Americans were pushing in from the opposite site and fervently hoped they would get here before the Russians. We hoped the war would be over soon in Berlin and everywhere. Thirteen and fourteen year old boys were now drafted to help save Berlin. They received a short training with guns, grenades and bayonets to be able to support the people at the home front. In addition they were supposed to hold back the Russians on one side and the Americans and British at our back. There were only old men, women and children and disabled people left in Germany and in no way could they even attempt to hold back any kind of military invasion. Our grandma from Berlin (Koenigswusterhausen) wrote in her letters that gunshots and grenade fire were heard every day now. Some Americans had settled into some suburbs of Berlin. There was almost no house in the area that had not been damaged or destroyed. Aunt Gloria's beautiful home had fallen to a grenade assault and had burned to the ground. At least the Nazis could not move in and live in it. The Villa Ruth, our friends house was also demolished and their beautiful yacht was sunk. Thank God grandma's little house was still standing and the boat house was in good shape. We were glad that the letter she wrote to us did not end up in the wrong hands. She would have been very much in trouble or even eliminated for writing us about war news. She also said that a truck with Hitler propaganda went down the road saying, "Fight to the last man. Berlin was not to be given up. We will survive!!" We were happy to have escaped from the hell hole that used to be our wonderful city.

Somehow we felt guilty that we had all we needed to eat and so many thousands of other children and old people had to starve. Hitler and his brute was hated vehemently in many families, but they were not allowed to voice their opinions because there were still fanatics around, believing Hitler will win that war.

There was one rumor that said the SS will come around to people delivering medication to people that would like to kill themselves or their children so they would not fall in to the hands of the enemy. According to statistics there were still around 100,000 children accounted for and thousands more unaccounted for living in the ruins of Berlin and many more in the railroad tunnels and in the underground.

Behind closed doors our grandparents and mom said now Hitler has totally snapped. Many people followed that advice from the SS, and the suicides began. People were so desperate for the misery to end.

We heard the Americans came to Strassburg. That meant they could be here in one or two days from France to Lichtenstein around Switzerland to Frankfurt on the Rheine. The Russians came from Czechoslovakia over Yugoslavia and Hungary. They could be here in a week or so. The news of their barbaric behavior went far ahead of them. Looting, destruction, rapes followed behind.

There were no such stories about the Americans. The reports about them were really good. They even shared their rations with many of those starving people and children. Soup kitchens were opened; blankets, boots and jackets were distributed. Care packages came by airplane all the way from America. We all wished the Americans would arrive in our area first.

One day we were awakened by the sound of grenades and gunfire flying overhead. Grandpa came and helped us to get dressed hurriedly. He handed us gas masks. We were astonished. Oh no, we cried. Has Berlin followed us here? Mom took our baby girl and rushed after us and our grandparents to the basement. Behind the hutch there was a door that we never had seen and did not know it existed. It let us all the way into the barn where there were bails of hey and straw. Grandpa pulled a hidden latch that opened into a tunnel, laid out with railroad ties. With a storm lantern in his hands he ordered us to follow him into a great chamber. The chamber was built into a rock and it looked like a grotto. In the ceiling were beams built to strengthen it. Grandpa whispered and said grinning, "Now they can come". Even a tank cannot penetrate our grotto. How often had we played in the backyard and never suspected that something like that was below us. Grandpa had built all this during the war. Before his retirement he had worked for the railroad as an engineer and the railroad ties were given to him as a supplement to his salary. He first planned to build a root cellar behind the barn but as conditions worsened, he built this bunker. Grandpa was digging very deep and all of a sudden fell into the grotto with his shovel and a bunch of dirt. He was very surprised to find himself in a great big grotto 12 feet underground, all rock, top to bottom. He put some columns and beams up, built some beds, a whole kitchen, a shelf space for the canned goods that grandma had prepared with moms help. The two women had to cook something up every day, meat vegetables and fruits, everything would be canned. If we had to live down there, he could feed us all for a long time. His motto was in war times you never know. He built chairs and a table. He stockpiled blankets and pillows and other bedding. Grandpa went to the market and got sugar, powdered milk, beans, noodles and a big container for drinking water. He had laid electricity and water pipes for a bathroom. Anything you could think of, he brought to the bunker. It was cold in the bunker even in the summer so he put an electric heater down below. Pots and pans, a radio, and even toys for us children. We were safe to talk and to hear music. The baby could cry without being heard. We would be safe and sound in that bunker.

Every day grandpa and grandma would have to go upstairs and feed the animals. They let Snuffi the dog roam free, the cat felt good in the barn, but the grandparents had to milk the goat and the sheep and feed the rabbits, pigs, geese and ducks. In order to stay down in the bunker my grandparents had to get rid of all the animals. Snuffi was sort of a little guard dog. He would bark and scare people out of the yard.

One day when our grandparents returned to our hiding placed later than usual, we got scared. But at their return they told us that the Americans had arrived. We did not have to worry because the foot soldiers were very friendly, shared food, Hershey chocolate, gum, crackers, and cigarettes with the

German people standing in the streets, waving white handkerchiefs and greeting them with handshakes. They had their guns over their shoulders and not pointed at the folks. We called the Americans Ami's for short. We were elated when grandpa told us that bunker time was over and the war is over. Let's celebrate the end of this barbaric time. We went outside to see with our own eyes how friendly they were.

The next morning we sat at the table for breakfast, a big tank drove by our kitchen window almost taking the downspout down, that's how close they came. Our kitchen window was open. We had nothing to fear anymore.

Slowly the hutch cover of the tank opened and I saw my first colored American looking out of the hole. He had a big grin on his face and the white in his eyes glistened in the sun. He had the whitest teeth that I had ever seen. He pointed at our table of breakfast food and made motions for us to continue eating. We all laughed. It was such a relief not to be frightened anymore. Two other friendly soldiers appeared out of the tank. Grandpa greeted them friendly and opened the door for them. They declined his invitation and urged us to finish our breakfast. The Ami's went back into the tank and drove off, taking our front fence down. It was no big deal, grandpa said. He would repair it. Just then the black fellow came running back and threw us a carton of cigarettes and some Hershey bars. We assumed that was to repay for the damage on the fence.

But to our regret the happiness of the Ami's arrival was short-lived. Here came the greedy Soviets (Russians). They demanded one third of Berlin and also the north part of Germany. The French and Americans had to concede to their demands so that placed us under the Russian command. They gave the Americans two weeks or so to vacate the area. Grandpa had to sell all the livestock in a hurry to be able to disappear with us down into the bunker. Grandpa had a side job since he retired from the railroad. He drove the hearse for a cemetery and had to care for the four black horses. He used the hearse to load all the animals in and bring them to the black market. In one day he sold them all and brought the horses and the hearse back. He told the funeral home owner he would go to see his daughter in Switzerland and was not sure if he would be back. The funeral director wished him good luck and they said their good byes. As grandpa came home he started to bring pictures and his favored tools down to the bunker, Grandma's wool yarn and her rocking chair, the featherbeds and then we were ready for the Russians to arrive.

Before Grandpa went down to the bunker where we all waited, he went to the neighbor's and told them also that he would bring his family to Switzerland. He went one more time to the mailbox on the fence and checked for mail. He saw on the end of the road a guy filthy and unkempt in rags, even rags around his feet walking like a drunk. This strange figure yelled, "the Russians are coming, hurry, hurry." Then that bundle of rags fell in grandpa's arms. "Oh Opa, said the person in rags. "Is it you Opa?" Grandpa helped him run to the bunker just before the Russians arrived in our street. Dad told grandpa that he was walking right ahead of the Russians for days, pretending he was a disabled person, because he had learned that Russians respected idiots and disabled people and even giving him food. Before he could tell us all his escape stories he had to clean up and eat first.

Dad had been seriously wounded in Russia when his tank was shot and exploded. He was rescued by a young Russian peasant who took him to his humble home and with his mother, nourished him back to health. That is all what our dad told us for the moment because the Russians came and filled the streets with terrifying noise. Dad said hopefully is everyone hiding their women and young girls. I have walked with them for weeks and know how terrible these Russians behave. They raped anything that had a skirt on. They molested children and old women for, too, this unruly brutes. For a few weeks they would torment and terrify everyone. Finely the commanders won the overhand and gave the command to let go of their violent behavior. They had to go to training to follow commands and to behave better. But many young girls and lots of women had been raped already. Mom, Inge and me were safe in grandpa's bunker. We had to stay for many weeks down below. We found out later that one of our young friends, a 13-year-old girl, was gang-raped by five Russian soldiers. The life of that girl was destroyed forever.

After a few weeks the guys became cabin-fever down in the bunker and wanted to check on how things were going up there. Dad knows that we would need new papers so he and grandpa prepared to go to the headquarters of the Russian commander. We needed a birth certificate for our baby Evie. Mom was frightened and did not want dad to go. Dad said, mom we have to start somewhere. It will be not good to stay for more weeks down here. If we do not get the proper papers as they told us on the radio we could be cut in an Russia home invasion where the Russians check for people without papers. We don't want to be subject to that and risk to be shipped to Siberia. Grandpa and dad went and did the right thing. In order to be a legal document it had to have the Soviet seal which was a hammer and a sickle. Mom was still afraid that the Russian commander would be indifferent to our dad. He was still young and had to be fighting against the Russians. Dad calmed her down and said everything will be right from now on. You have to understand mom many of this soldiers had no military training. They were herded up from farms and far away villages, even some were Normand's never lived in civilization, just put together for the long march to Germany. Without uniforms or boots, plan sheepskin around their feet held together by a leather strap. Alone that sight of them frightened people.

After months of training and established learning to follow commands, their appearance improved a little. Their sadistic behavior was now subject to punishment. Many of the Normand's out of the deepest Mongolian dessert were completely uncivilized, had no respect for anybody or anything. They had to learn to conform under the severest circumstances in their war-ridden and poverty stricken homeland. They were wild, untrained and seemingly without souls. The sign and the news of this unruly group frightened us enough to retreat to our underground shelter, our place of safety. Grandpa forced to sell all his livestock in order not to have to feed and milk them. We did not want anyone to follow him and discover us.

After grandpa retired from the railroad he had a side job at a mortuary. He had to the use of the hearse and four wonderful black horses. He used the hearse to transport the animals to the black market. There they sold immediately because there was still great hunger among the people. He came home around lunch time and had everything sold. A big bundle of money and some other goods he had bought.

Grandma and mom had preserved meat and canned goods which was stored in the bunker. The cats and dogs were in crates now down in the shelter. The whole house looked deserted. Grandpa and dad moved the hutch back in its place blocking the door and came in to the air shaft which was hidden under a bush. Before going underground they told neighbors that we were going to Switzerland to where one of grandpa's daughters lived. No one knew where we really were.

Later on as we came out of the bunker we found our house in disarray. Furniture and everything from the kitchen were gone. Water faucets ripped out the walls. Our clothes strewn on the floor. One old closet they had used as a toilet, what a bad smell in that room. Toilets and sinks lay broken on the floor. We were told that the Russians were not used to our culture and had never seen a water closet, a bucket or water faucets coming out of the wall. Only the folks in the cities had higher life styles and know more about these commodities.

As dad and grandpa got to the headquarters, he run by sheer accident in to Ivan his lifesaver in Russia. Ivan yelled "Bert, Bert my friend." He hugged and kissed him on both cheeks as it is custom in Russia. When dad was rescued by Ivan in Russia they had decided on the name Bert for our dad because Gerhard was too hard to say for Kalinka, Ivan's mom and Herbert, was dad's middle name and for short it would be Bert. Dad had learned so much of the Russian language that he really could talk to Ivan. He told him he was captured and was shipped to Siberia for longer than a year. He was able to learn a lot about Russia and the language and the culture. He had escaped out of the war camp and made his way back to civilization dressed as a bum and behaving as an idiot. Running in to some soldiers of the Russian army they made him their mascot. Ivan introduced dad to his commander and praised him as a good tailor. The commander liked dad too and offered him a job to tailor for them. Only one day later a truck arrived with sewing machines and lots of material. As Ivan saw in what misery the house was, he ordered furniture for the whole house. The kitchen got all the pots and pans we would need. We got curtains, bed wash, pillows, blankets, and everything a family needs to live in comfort. Thank you Ivan, you really had a big heart.

Ivan and the commander brought on the clientele, too. Generals and officers had their uniforms made by dad and mom. Often they got us food and gallons of vodka, what dad could offer the clients when they ordered their outfits. Whenever a client entered the house he was greeted properly and offered a glass of vodka that meant a kiss on both cheeks and the drink was the custom in Russia. So they would feel home said Ivan. Orders came in by the dozens and mom and dad were very busy. All the material that was left over dad could use for us. The Russian clients brought us lots of money, sometimes a whole backpack full. Mom and grandma stored the money in one of the dressers; it had five drawers and was stuffed full. Dad's desk filled up with bank notes too. We also had to put some of the money in suitcases. We could only be grateful to Ivan that he had send a crew to restore all the damage in the house, gave us wonderful furniture and brought us clients so we could start a new beginning. There was still hunger around us and we felt guilty to have so plenty. Often Ivan and the commander (Peter) came to our house for social hour. They always brought food and drinks as it is Russian custom when you visit friends. They often drank and talked far into the night after the women and children went to bed.

Now after the war there were very few men left in our city. Many were killed, some still in war camps. Ivan and the commander Peter wanted dad to go in to politics and work hand-in-hand with the Russian regime. They trusted and respected our dad and needed people to help to get Germany back on its feet.

Dad was given a position similar to a Mayor of our city, Schleiz in Thueringen. He was also the founder of the first party after the war and it was called CSU, short for Christian Social Union. With that position came a big house with conference room and an office for dad, a car which was a Mercedes convertible, brown and cream in color. All of a sudden we were on top of the world again. It was said that we had to move away from grandma and grandpa but we were only a mile away. Even

Inge my sister and I could go to see them often and we spent weekends if mom and dad had to go out. We had also help in our household now. Our helper was Christa. She came right out of the camp in Dachau and needed a new start just as we did. She still had no hair because they cut hair so short in the camps that it almost needed a year to grow back. She was very sweet but she also told us what she has suffered at the concentration camp. She was Jewish and had lost her whole family in Dachau.

Dad and mom had to attend many political events or parties. Christa tucked us in to bed and told us all the hair-raising stories that Jewish people had to endure under Hitler in the camps. We learned a lot form her. I made notes often so I would not forget the horrible stories. Somehow the written notes were lost but they were etched in my mind indelicately. Our Aunt Hildegard and cousin Christa lived in the middle of town where Hildegard operated a hair salon. Christa was learning the trade. Our grandparents and mom had always invited Hildegard and Christa to come to the bunker for safety but the invitation would never be attended. Hildegard would never abandon her clients or her salon with all the tools. Both women stuck it out in their own house. Thank God nothing ever happened to them. In the center of town it was slightly safer for people. The headquarters were nearby and the chance of being found out was greater. In spite of our age difference we got along well with Christa our cousin. When she did special demonstrations of her work for examinations and tests Inge and I were her models. That meant we have got all the free haircuts, shampoos and conditioners we needed. Sometimes Aunt Hildegard did special elaborate hairdos for weddings, parties, or so. She often used our mom as a model.

My sister Inge and I were trained in a dance group. We had very good and strong voices so we would get speech and singing lessons. We were put in an entertainer group because we were checked out for our talents and we were good in what we did. All children in our show were tested for their talents and that made it fun for us to go there. It was custom by the Soviets to belong to a special group. There were mathematic clubs, writer clubs, sport and dance clubs. We had to stay in classes all day and got lunch from government. We learned a lot, had we missed so much during the air raids we caught up fast with the new Soviet school system. We learned the Russian language so we could sing Russian folk songs and perform on stage. At first we had plays only in our school but as we spoke the language better and learned Russian folk dances we were invited in other cities and schools to perform there. It came easily to us and we had lots of fun.

Sometimes we organized shows and plays with other children of our age group. We became so adept that we often played at the community center and competed with other schools. Later on we entertained adults and children in many cities and Russian leaders, too, in shows we had put together on our own.

Our hero Mom. From left, Inge (13 years), Helga (12 years), Mom (31 years), Baby Bernd (1 year), Evie (5 years), Gerhard (9 years). At this time, we fled through the white water River Saale to the west to the City of Halle. June 1950

Inflation

I was about 9 or 10 years old, the war was over and I was thinking we were rich. Everything drawer, suitcase and even in boxes were bundled bank notes. All that money it seemed to be crazy. Our mom went to go shopping and she got a backpack full of notes to go get bread, butter and some lunch meat. Thousands of marks she spent for three items. Mom, dad and grandma and grandpa sat down for a meeting. They were talking about a recession. What is a recession? I looked it up in the dictionary. It means the money is not worth much anymore. You had to pay obscene amounts of money for the goods you needed. So one day we all went to the shoe store and picked out some boots and shoes for all of us. Grandpa had a wagon, like a goat cart, which was loaded with gunny sacks. In the sacks were money in bundles of hundreds, fifties, tens and five mark notes. He pulled the little wooden cart in to the store and the store owner and grandpa started counting the money since we were still trying on shoes. When we were done grandpa had only a handful of notes left. All gunny sacks were empty. The next day we did the same thing. Loading up sacks of money, going to the meat factory in our city, loading the cart up with ham and salami, we had five big hams and ten salamis for two sacks of money. We still had so much money at home. Dad and grandpa went to the men's store and got brand new suits and shirts, blazers and fancy ties. They spent lots of money for it. Then mom, grandma and the children went to the store and we all got complete outfits from top to bottom. It cost an arm and a leg but we had it. Dad had worked so hard for the Russians, Ivan and his commanders and they had paid him like a king. Opa had sold everything, fruit, corn, tobacco, rabbits, ducks, honey, milk from the goats, homemade cheese from the goats. This all had helped to save up lots of money. We did not have to spend money on groceries. Grandpa's little farm provided us with everything except sugar, salt, pepper and paprika. So we had lots of money saved up. But why are we spending it all at once now? We finally had our dresser drawers back for our clothing. Suitcases were empty and only a small amount was left for emergency. One day we had to turn all our money in to the bank. The government wanted to change the Reich's mark into Deutsch mark. All the money we had was not worth a dime anymore. Mom and dad brought it all to the bank. They were hoping to get a percentage for the amount they brought in but they were really surprised to get 41.00 Deutsch mark per head. What do you do with such a small sum? Mom was upset we could tell. But mom was very surprised when she went to the store and a bread would cost only one Deutsch mark and not some 1,000 Reich's mark anymore. Now you could buy lots of things for only pennies. Dad was still working for his Russian friend and he must have known what would happen to our money and that is why we went crazy shopping and spending as much money as possible, so not everything was lost. Thanks to Ivan again. Now dad got paid for all his sewing in Deutsch mark and the Russians had to learn to count out the new money. The sewing jobs came in a lot slower and we heard dad and grandpa say its is not enough to live on anymore. But Ivan and his commander had a new job for dad. The city needed a Mayor. The Russians trusted our dad and put him in to this position. Headquarters organized everything for him. All the papers had to be signed. Arrangements were made for an office and a bigger house. We had to move. Oh what a painful decision. But they found us a house only a mile from our grandparents house. We could just walk there two days a week after school and on evenings when mom and dad had to go to meetings or a party. Dad even got a car, a Mercedes convertible, chocolate and cream was the color. Wonderful! For a few years, we were on top of the hill until everything fell apart.

Dad had to flee in the middle of the night. We had to move out of the big house into a two bedroom poor house, a homeless shelter. Our whole world came crushing down again.

Mom and even Inge and I were ordered to the headquarters and were investigated by the Russian commanders. But we did not know where our dad was and we had no contact with him. So we could honestly talk about it!

Another Upheaval in Our Lives

One morning Inge and I came down from our bedroom, two little girls awaiting their breakfast. We were stunned to see mom all upset and red-eyed from crying. She told us that our dad had to flee from the Soviets, over to the west sector where they could not find him. He had said something in a meeting that the Russian commander misunderstood or not liked. He only got his overnight case, that was always packed for emergencies, like going to another city to speak where he had to stay overnight then. One extra shirt, one pair of socks, some underwear and a jacket was in that suitcase. He picked it up, gave mom a kiss and a very short explanation and went off.

Mom could not even tell us the whole story she was so overcome with grief, shaking and weeping. Suddenly we were interrupted by a group of Soviet soldiers banging on our front door. Making noises, yelling open, open! We were afraid and hid in the kitchen. Mom had to open the door or they would break it down. The Russians went through the house like ruffians, breaking everything in their way. Lamps, vases, our telephone flew to the floor and broke. They went from top to bottom of our home in a very rude way.

A truck was stopping in front of the house, all our household things were taken from the house to be loaded onto the truck. Even our beds, only our clothes were not taken and a few blankets. Some cosmetics and hairdryer and brushes were dumped onto the floor. A soldier brought some boxes and told us to put our things into the boxes and left.

Stunned we stood watching our belongings being hauled away. We were so stunned we could not move. Dad's Mercedes was towed away and in a few hours we had lost everything we had owned and were left standing in an empty house. Not even a chair to sit on.

In the utility room mom found an old table where she used to fold laundry on. No doubt, it was too old and not desirable for the soldiers to take so we had a table. Mom went and locked the front door which the soldiers had left wide open. We went out to our backyard and got the little bench next to the pond and brought it inside. Then we sat down and had a good cry, each of us for a different reason. Myself for being left behind by dad without a good bye, it really hurt me. We missed school that day and that was good because the truck came back around noon and the driver, a German guy explained to us, we had to get all our stuff together and had to leave the house. He had to bring us down the street to a warehouse with a little house on the side which would now be our home.

On my way to school I had to pass that warehouse every time and often did wonder what would be in that little house. Now I found out. We had a guard standing in front of our new home right after we were done moving. The guard would be changed every four hours and we were not allowed to go outside. Days went by and we missed so much school. We missed our dance group, our friends, our speech and our singing lessons. We would have given anything to play outside.

One day mom was ordered to the headquarters. They told her that she could go to jail if she would keep the whereabouts of our dad from them. She told them she didn't know or had no contact with him. We really were clueless. We had visitors, grandpa and grandma came to see us. The Russian soldiers had come to their house and checked there for our dad. In the little house was furniture from the former owner. They must have fled from the Soviets. Mom asked grandma if she would get us an extra set of dishes and some utensils. The ones in the house were not very appetizing. Cups and plates were chipped and forks bend and so forth. Grandpa brought us all the things we could dream of, even toys. Good food from their pantry. He wanted us to come back to his house, there would be more room but the Soviets held us there.

Aunt Hildegart came to see us. She was stunned that they would not let us children go to school. She wrote a petition and let all her clients sign it. We children had not done anything to the Russians and why did we have to suffer and even were held back from school. The Russian commander had a hearing with us and after we promised we had no contact with our dad, we were allowed to go back to school. What a change, we would see our friends and classmates. We could walk the one mile to school. The air was so fresh and wonderful, we were free. We still lived in shame, the Soldiers were still watching us, but we had won some of our freedom back. The surveillance went on for a whole year and then they gave up.

The little house had only two bedrooms and we had to double up. Inge and I and Evie were in one room. Gerhard slept in the living room. Bernd, the baby with mom in the other bedroom. People whispered behind our backs, that is the wife or the children of the traitor. It was really hard on us. We loved our dad and they called him a deserter or traitor. What had he done?

The house was really crowded when it rained and we could not go outside. We had no friends coming to the little house because it looked so poor. We stayed in school almost the whole day, took every class we could just not to go home. We were back on stage with our group, dancing and singing as if nothing happened. Children adjust sometimes fast. Seldom people wanted to know if we had heard of the spy from West Germany, we had not. One whole year went by and one day we had nobody watching us anymore. Another day and nobody showed up, maybe it was over we hoped. And after no guard showed up for more than a week, we knew it was over.

Our grandparents wanted us to come to their house on one weekend after the watch post had left. Mom had made us all new clothes. We had a picture taken by a photographer in town and after that we went to the grandparents' house. What a surprise to see all mom's brothers and sisters with all their families there. What a get together that was. We were so happy to see all the little ones running and playing all over the lawn and the living room keeping us children busy. The grown ups sat in groups and talked. They all hugged and kissed mom again and again. That made me think something is going on but what? I could not find out on that weekend.

There is a little city, the name is Hirschberg in Thueringen. A river goes by the city, the name is Saale. It is a strong white water river. The border from East to West Germany that means Soviet sector and American sector. Whoever wanted to go to the West German sector had to cross the little bridge. On one side of the bridge was the guard house with the patrol of the Russians on the other side the Americans and their guard house. You needed a pass to cross the bridge. If someone wanted to flee, they would have to go directly through the river. Posts were only 200 feet away from each other on the Soviet side. Four times a day they would be replaced by other Soviet soldiers. The city had a leather factory, and many people went to see the factory. People could buy purses, shoes, gloves or just go and visit the factory. The building was about a block away from the river so many people went along to see the river bank and the big boulders in the stream. Many of them checked out if there would be a way to cross the river to get away from the Soviets and live in peace in West Germany, the American sector. The city across the river was Halle and many refugees ended up in Halle, West Germany. They called it the Golden West. The city we would see one day and be reunited with our dad again, hopefully.

One day we too made the trip to the leather factory. We did not know but mom had her reasons she said. We were really taken by the smell of the part of the factory where they cleaned the hides. In other parts we saw women sewing purses, gloves and in another part men made the shoes on big machines. For lunch we went down to the river, sitting on boulders and having our sandwich. The river bank was very steep and we saw foam hitting the rocks in the water. The river was very loud too, when the water was gushing on the rocks and pearls of foam went in the air. On the way home mom was very quiet.

One day we put on our new clothes, got a haircut and everyone put on their new shoes from Hirschberg Leather Factory. Aunt Hildegard and Christa gave us our haircuts and Aunt hugged and kissed us. How funny, that never happened before. That was very unusual because they were more on the cooler side and hugs and kisses we got only from the grandparents. All the six years we lived there we could not remember being hugged and kissed like that. Strange! Something is going on. As we came home to our little house where we had to move to, after the Russians confiscated our big house and made us move out in such a hurry. Grandma and grandpa came to visit. Mom had picked up the pictures and gave them to grandma, all of a sudden grandma was crying. Why? What was that all about? Grandpa had to wipe a tear away too. What was going on? Did anything happen to dad? Did they have news? Something was not right. I finally could not hold back anymore and insisted that mom tell me what was going on. Mom told Inge and me we will go and see dad. Was there any news? Did we get a pass to go over the bridge? We had to promise mom, not to talk to anyone about it. It was a Saturday and we had no school so we saw no one of our friends and could not talk about it to anyone. On Sunday morning we had to pack our backpacks leaving everything behind and everyone we loved. Sister Inge and I had to sleep in one bed that night. That was always that way when we were frightened, we clang to each other. We held on to each other for dear life and cried ourselves to sleep. Inge is 13 years old and I a tender 12.

Early in the morning we went to the bus to Hirschberg on the Saale, the river in Thueringen, Germany. It was the 12th of June 1950. The sun came up like every other day, not letting us know what would happen that day. Our hearts were heavy, and we cried for Oma and Opa. We would not see them for a long, long time. Mom told us stories of her life to kill the time on the bus ride, some funny, some not. She did not want us to get too sad about our departing. We had to listen to the advice she gave us to get over the river. We had to use our backpacks to sit on, sliding down the river bank. When we would arrive down on the water we would have to put the backpacks on our back to save the papers and the little things we were taken with us to the West. Mom would take our baby brother Bernd. Inge would hold on to Eve, 5 years old at the time. Helga you hold on to your younger brother Gerhard, 9 years old, said mom. Now on the way down Evie fell out of the grip of Inge. Mom gave the baby Bernd to Inge and grabbed Evie so she would not scream and alarm the post that guarded the Russian side of the river. One more time mom told us how much she loved us and then we had to jump in to the river. The power of the water was so strong that it would take us under. We had to fight for our life. The water was ice cold and we all cried. Mom too. She yelled go on we have to make it or we will be shot by the post that guarded the Soviet side of the river. Go on! Go on! Go, go my children! We were almost in the middle of the river when Inge lost our baby brother through the waves. The little guy was bobbing out of the water, going down and coming up again on a different spot. Mom grabbed him in the last minutes before he drowned. The commotion was to great not to be missed by the Soviet guard. He started shooting at us, the bullets hitting the rocks and the water around us. Mom yelled, go faster! We can make it! We are almost there! Suddenly we saw blood in the water around mom's legs but she pushed us forward. The Russians cannot shoot anymore if we reach the other side.

People came running down the river bank on the west side, the American sector, yelling and waving, come on, you made it, come on, faster! We were totally exhausted from the fight with the water. We fell to the ground and people had to carry us the last stretch out of the river. We made it! Mom's leg was bleeding bad. The people had called for an ambulance already. They brought blankets and clothing to the rivers edge to make us warm up. Most of our clothing was ripped off by the river. We were practically arriving naked at the Golden West. But we made it.

Now we were to see our dad. We waited but he was not there. He waited on a different spot, where it would have been safer for us to cross. The police car went down the river to find him. Mom in the meantime refused to be carried away by the ambulance. She would stay with us until dad was found. There he was all of a sudden, getting out of the police car. He went on his knees to hug and kiss us all. The Red Cross came and took care of us while mom and dad went in to the ambulance. We stayed with the Red Cross, got hot schokolade and some sandwiches, got nice dry clothing and they put us up in a tent on the lawn with some cots in there to let us rest until mom and dad came back. We huddled together on one cot and fell asleep.

End of winter 1949-1950. Little baby Bernd shortly before we fled, in a high-chair convertible. (Last picture of the little house.)

The Camps

Dad awakened us after they came back from the hospital. Dad said we will go and get a hotel room so we could celebrate that we were all together now. But immigration officers arrived and had a different idea.

We had lost all our papers in the water. They were in one of the backpacks ripped away from the stream. Without papers nobody goes anywhere in Germany (bureaucracy). The Officers loaded us up in a Volkswagon van, asked dad if he would like to come with us because he had papers and was free to go. Dad stayed with us and they brought us to a camp for people that crossed the river before us and were waiting for papers to move on.

The camp was a big warehouse. There were bunk beds. For privacy they hung some blankets between the bunks. There was a mess hall and we stood in line to receive our meals. We stood in line to see a doctor and stood in line to take showers. There were no accommodations for children. We had to sit on the bunks or stand in line for something. Two weeks we lived like that. That was the Golden West, mom asked? We had to be immunized and debriefed and saw a shrink.

One day we were put on a bus and brought in to another camp. End station for the next six years. Raitersaich was the name of the camp in Bavaria. Americans built it as they arrived in Germany. They had moved out into a headquarters in Ansbach and Nutenberg. The barracks had one or two bedrooms, a living area and a kitchen. Ten units to a barrack. There were army beds, blankets, pillows, towels, some pots and pans, some closets, some cupboards but no water or a toilet. The water was on the end of a hallway. The toilets were in a community building like an outhouse type, ten holes in a row. Mom almost freaked out. Bathrooms with showers, 15 in a row without privacy. Women had their day for showers and men too. Children could be bathed in a tub in the kitchen. We bathed in our kitchen in a small tub for six long years. We had some papers after a while but could still not move out of the camp because we had to see a shrink for having been brainwashed by the Russians. And after one year in the camp our little sister Monika was born. That made us a family with six children on one income from our poor dad. He went with a suite case of goods from house to house selling shoestrings, soaps, needles and elastic rubber bands, thread and things. We all loved Monika very much. She had hazel eyes and blonde curls all over. She was just lovely and sweet. Other people moved away from the camp as they found work and apartments but we were stuck in the camp. Dad could not find us normal housing. I overheard him telling mom they would rather take people with dogs as tenants than a family with so many children. Mom said it is alright, we have each other and the children have a good school here. There was a church also which we could use even if we were Lutheran. Our time will come.

Monica (4 years) and Evie (10 years) in Camp Raitersaich.

Our first friends in the Refugee Camp. From left: Hilder Anger, Helga (17 years), Papa (39 years), Mom (35 years), Maria Burkhard (Monika's Godmother).

Mom (27 years old) "showing off".
The first car (Mercedes) in the Camp.

New Year's Celebration at Camp Raitersaich. 1951.
From left: Maria and Hors Burkhard, Mom and Dad in our living room.

First day of school at the Camp. 1955.
Third from the left in the front row, Brother Bernd.

Russia – Siberia

Our dad told us his story about Russia.

I woke up, pain went through my whole body, he said. I heard the howling of wolves. They could not get to me because I was hanging over a big branch of a tree. How did I get here, he tried to remember. Nothing in my head was working. He told he saw the snow below the tree and some red spots. That was his own blood dripping out of him. He was unable to move because the pain was to great. He said he did not feel the bitter cold, only pain everywhere. He went unconscious again. He woke up one more time and was happy the wolves could not get him. As he woke up again he found himself lying on a bed in a room, not a hospital bed or room. When he opened his eyes he saw a woman. The woman tried to feed him some soup. There was someone else in the room on the other side of the bed holding dad's head steady. A young man smiling friendly. Dad asked, where am I? He moved a little while asking the question. A strong stab of pain went through his body. Both the women and the young man held their hands over their mouth to show him not to speak or to move. Dad said he still could not remember where he was and what had happened.

For the longest time he just laid there falling in and out of consciousness and having enormous amounts of pain. Dad was fighting a fever and was relieved when he felt something cold on his body. One day he woke up and felt a little better. The women came and washed him. He noticed a big bandage made of a bed sheet around his upper body. He knew that was where all his pain came from. He had not seen the wound yet but had certainly felt it. Dad as asking himself how did I get here? How long have I been here? Who are these people? All these questions and no answers. He heard the women talking to the young man, she called him Ivan, that must be his name. He called the woman Mamuschka, that must be her name.

Dad slowly remembered that he was in a tank with three other soldiers. Where were his comrades? He faintly remembered hanging on a tree branch and wolves heading up the tree. After some time he remembered more and more about a terrible explosion. Dad remembered metal pieces sticking out of the snow. That must have been from the tank. The explosion must have blown him out of the tank and into the tree. He was in Russia, lying in a bed, covered with a bear skin. The two people caring for him, speaking a language he never had heard before. Ivan and Mamuschka came in to his room, both of them smiling from ear to ear. They tried to put him in a sitting position. It made him scream in pain but it got better after they let go of him.

Mamuschka opened up the bandage and washed the blood away, put a new sheet around the wound and let him sleep some more. All of a sudden dad woke up feeling hungry like a bear. He smelled food being prepared in the kitchen. Soup or stew, whatever Mamuschka prepared smelled very good. He was more aware of his body now and was embarrassed that he wore a diaper. Who had put that on him? He hoped that it was Ivan. Dad could not get up yet, it was very hard to get into a sitting position. Those wonderful people massaged his legs, his arms, and after weeks when he felt more healed, even his back. The wound in his upper body was not infected anymore. He had to move his arms which made the big wound still hurt a lot. Dad was wondering how long he was laying here? Days? Weeks?

After he was awake more often Mamuschka and Ivan sat with him, tried to speak or making signs and gestures with their hands to make themselves understood. Ivan had a piece of paper with all kinds of marks on it. After a while dad started counting those marks. He was sure they meant how many days he had been there already. He thought that he had been awake only once or twice and was amazed that he counted 18 marks already. So he had been there 18 days and could remember only a couple. Mamuschka had many times put ice on this chest to bring the fever down. It finally subsided.

When they came to his room they had bread or a cup of coffee in their hand, pointing at it and said a word, the Russian name for bread or the cup, water or coffee. They made him repeat all the words until he had them in his memory so he could ask them for what he needed in the Russian language.

The day came when they helped him out of bed. He got so dizzy that he fell right back onto the bed. His legs were so shaky but they both kept on forcing him to get up and take a few steps. After trying very hard and holding onto Ivan, dad walked around in the room. It still took days for him to get out of the bed by himself.

Dad was aware that he had not shaved in weeks and his beard was kind of itchy. But that was a smaller evil. He had detected many small wounds on his legs and feet. They still hurt when he had to walk.

One day Mamuschka and Ivan were sitting by his side, pointing to Ivan. Mamuschka made the sign of a cradle, to make dad understand that Ivan was her son. She pointed to herself and said Kalinka, pointed again and repeated Kalinka. From that day on dad called her Kalinka, not Mamuschka any longer because he understood that Mamuschka probably meant mother.

Dad had not seen the house yet, only the one room he was confined to for so long. Day by day encountered more of the house. Coming out of his room he walked into what you could call a combination of living room and kitchen. From there two doors went on to Ivan's room and the other to a room you could call a bathroom. There was not water toilet, only a chair with a hole and a bucket underneath. Ivan showed him that he could relieve himself there and some fresh snow would be covering it up. The bucket would be emptied several times a day and then filled with fresh snow.

Kalinka (Mamouschka) had to bring snow in for cooking instead of water. The outside pump was frozen. She used snow for making tea in the big samovar (Russian tea pot) that was constantly sitting on the fireplace.

Dad was pointing to Kalinka asking with hand signs where she was sleeping. She pointed to Ivan's room. In Ivan's room was only a very small cot and a shelf for clothing. Dad saw for the first time how poor these two people were.

After some time he asked Ivan where he slept and Ivan pointed to the bench around the fireplace. Dad concluded that they had given him, a stranger and on top of that the enemy, the best bed and room in the house. How in the world can I ever repay them for what they have done for me, thought dad.

One day dad felt very good. Ivan took him out of the house. There was a shed and not another house as far as he could see. Only snow, lots of snow. Ivan opened the door to the shed, from the rafters hung salt meat and many hides. Dad saw deer, wolf and even bear hides. Dad was thinking that Ivan had shot the wolves first before getting him out of that tree.

Dad had only a t-shirt on from Ivan and a blanket hanging around his shoulders. He saw his uniform jacket and pants all in shreds hanging from a wash line. He came back into the house, taking the rest of his uniform with him.

Dad made signs of sewing to Kalinka and she understood his gestures giving him a big sewing basket. He found everything he needed. Dad was sewing patches on his pants from the shredded jacket. It must have turned out very good because Kalinka was clapping her hands and dancing around laughing. Dad pointed to the blanket, she nodded and he went to work. Cutting the blanket up to be a jacket. He was sewing all the cut pieces together, slipped into it and surprised the lady of the house tremendously. He cut off the buttons of his uniform, sewing them onto his new outfit. Ivan could not believe what he saw and brought him another blanket. He pointed out to make a longer coat, like an overcoat. Dad stitched it all together like a cape because there was not enough material for making sleeves. But it did look well and was very warm, too.

Kalinka gave dad a sheepskin to make himself a hat. He wore the hat after it was done and all three were laughing and clapping their hands.

Dad still had not had a chance to shave. He had not looked into a mirror for a long time. Finally Kalinka gave him an old spotty mirror and dad could not believe it was him that looked back out at him. His hair had grown long and his beard was inches long. He was a mess. He was afraid of himself. He had to get better fast.

These people were so poor and giving him all the best. Having another mouth to feed must have been very hard on them. Dad was so grateful, they had saved his life, treating him like a king from the little bit they had for themselves. Wonderful, loving people. Thank God for them and for their generosity.

Dad started helping around the house as soon as he felt better. On the outside too whatever had to be done. He found some shingles in the shed and some tools. Maybe from Ivan's dad or so. They repaired the roof of the house and the shed. From bedsheets he made a nice dress for Kalinka and out of a couple of wolf skins a coat. It was so pretty it made her cry.

For Ivan he made a jacket out of wolf skins and also put the skin side on the outside and the fur inside so it looked like a nice leather jacket but was a lot warmer.

One day dad found some piles of planks behind the shed, nice oak wood. Since in the house the rooms had only stamped dirt floors dad looked for some tools in the shed and found to his surprise, everything he needed. There must have been at one time a handyman in that house. Dad and Ivan put wood floors in all the rooms. Kalinka was crying, laughing and dancing around so dad knows he did the right thing. He house was a lot warmer now.

As long as dad was in Kalinka's house there were no visitors. Nobody came to see them. Dad did not know if that was always so or if there were visitors sometimes. Maybe they intentionally lived out here in the wilderness because Ivan was a hunter?

There were so many questions, all unanswered, because of the language barrier.

It became time to move on. He was healed, his body was in a good condition. He wanted to get home. He did not want to put any more strain on those poor people. He made signs to wave good bye and they understood.

Kalinka made a nice meal, lots of meat, gave him some vodka and let him sleep one more night. In the morning he got dressed, had breakfast with both of them and saw signs of tears on both of their faces. Dad said he had to cry too.

Kalinka embraced him and gave him a kiss on either cheek like it is custom in Russia. After he went outside to see Ivan, dad realized that Ivan was all dressed up too so he would see him off. In front of the house was a sled loaded with furs. Ivan made signs to dad to slip in between the skins. Dad thought he would walk but was thinking Ivan had a reason to hide him under the furs. He knew if anyone would have seem him with Ivan they both would be dead. They went for two days and two nights letting dad out for little breaks. He never saw a village but this was okay with him. It would get Ivan in trouble if someone would see them. Ivan stopped the sled and led dad out, gave him a field bottle with water mixed with vodka so it would not freeze, gave him a pouch with food Kalinka had packed for him. Ivan put his arms around dad's shoulders, kissed him like his mother did and said dosvidanja, what probably meant good bye or good luck Dad was all alone. Ivan had made him a map in the snow and left. Siberia—Moscow—Germany.

They had a drink of vodka together, and that was their good-bye. Dad starting walking for hours and hours until he had to sit down and rest. He had something of Kalinka's food and some water mixed with vodka. After three days and nights walking without much sleep he run out of food and water. He said he was so tired but could not lay down to sleep or he would have frozen to death. Now and then he sat down for a while and napped a little, got up and kept on walking. He kept warm by running and flapping his arms and jumping after getting up from one of his naps. He eventually went near signs of civilization, at that time it did not matter to him anymore if this were Russians or Germans. He was at his end and did not care anymore. He stumbled more than he walked in to a group of German's from a battalion that was also lost and had no telephone contact anymore with any other German company. They were almost ready to take off back toward Germany. They fed him, let him shave, gave him a haircut and a new pair of boots, let him go on a cot and told him he had to get up early in the morning because they would take off for home. He was happy to hear his own language after months and went to sleep. Surrounded by trucks was a tent that had a cannon oven spitting out heat in all directions keeping everyone warm. In the morning dad would be debriefed on his encounter with the enemies. Dad would tell his commander as much as he knew about the attack on the tank and that he was the only one that got away. Dad found out that it was the end of April already, the winter had not let up in this icy country.

The other soldiers were happy because they could be home in a couple of weeks. They sat around telling their stories, having a beer and feeling good before they went to bed.

Early in the morning the picture had changed, their battalion was overrun by the Russians. There was no killing but everybody got loaded up on to the Russian army trucks. They were sent to Siberia. Five days and nights they were traveling on these trucks, now and then stopping for pit stops. They were fed dry bread and dry meat and given some water also mixed with vodka so the water would not freeze. The Russians did not push them around or hit them, just made sure that all went back onto the trucks. On the fifth day it was snowing and cold. One of the trucks got stuck. Everybody got out of the trucks and tried pushing the vehicle back on the tracks. It would not move. One Russian guy came with a blanket and put it under the wheels. That did the trick. They could continue to roll on. Now sitting on a covered truck by zero temperatures lets your feet and hands get very cold or even frozen.

Most of the POWs took their boots off and massaged their feet and hands. After they were done massaging their hands went under their arm pits so dad did like them to keep the hands warm. What helped for the cold too, that they had to sit so close together, like herring in a can said dad. Finally they arrived in a camp. It was a big camp, about 30-40 barracks. One big hospital, storage sheds and what was most remarkable was there were no guards to see on the outside. Dad remembered all the way to that camp they had not seen any villages or any houses but once they saw a freight train.

Arriving at the camp every newcomer had to drop their clothing, which would be burned in a big campfire. The men would get clothing from the camp with the barrack number on the jacket.

The pants were too big; dad had to use a piece of clothesline for a belt. Many others did the same as dad too, in order to hold the pants up. The sleeves were too long and many had to pull them back all the time. Dad saw all this as work possibilities coming up for him. There were groups of people put together for certain jobs. Some guys were commanded up to kitchen duty, the kitchen was in a separate barracks, close to the hospital.

Trucks brought in all necessary supplies needed in the camp. Dad counted one time about one hundred people to one barracks. Now and then there were fights, mostly between the polish people. They just could not get along and had a short temper. There was no intervention from the Russian posts situated in the back of each barracks in a room with one big, glass window to verse the on goings in the barracks. The guards usually just laughed and looked the other way.

There was one attraction in the camp and that was a woman doctor. You could see on doctor day how long the line was. Every one sick or not went to see her. Dad had still trouble with shrapnel metal in his feet. The doctor checked for any infections and gave him some lotion.

After a while, dad got fed up with pushing those long sleeves back all the time. He asked for a pair of scissors and a needle and thread, and he got all of that from one of the guards. He created a job for himself. All the guys had needs for a tailor. They paid him with some of their rations or cigarettes; some even gave him Russian money.

Word got around like wildfire that dad could sew. His clientele got bigger and bigger. The Russian guard and even the doctors and lab workers gave him things to fix. Almost all Russian people paid him with ruble, the Russian currency.

There was no store; you could not buy anything with that money. Dad took it anyway and saved it up. Nobody would steal it because there was no use for it.

He finally found out why there were no guards outside of the camp. If people wanted to run away the guards would just let them go. After a couple of days a truck would go back out to search for the person that fled. Most of the time they brought him back frozen. The campfire would be lit and the remains put on the fire. All camp occupants had to go out to the fire. Nobody was allowed to go back inside the barracks until the whole body was burned to ashes. The smell made many people nauseated. What a gruesome way to enforce obedience.

One truck driver delivering food heard about dad's sewing talents. He came to see him. Dad had learned a little of the Russian language from Ivan and Kalinka. He got evening lessons from one of the posts. He paid him with cigarettes for the lessons. Cigarettes were always a good bargaining tool.

When the truck driver came to dad he was able to understand what the guy wanted. He told dad he was going to get married. Dad would sew him a suit. The driver also asked dad if he would be able to sew a dress for the bride. Now dad had not seen the girl and would never see her. He told the groom to measure his bride's shoulders, her length and chest and also her midsection. Measure each part with a string and bring it back with the materials for the dress. The groom did so. When the groom brought the materials it was not what we would use for a wedding dress. He brought a bolt of wonderful woven (brocade?). The bride had put a picture out of a magazine article into the bag of materials and the silk thread she wanted him to use to sew with.

Dad needed a model and a young German POW had just the right measurements. He stood on a table to model the dress. He had quite some fun out of this cross dressing. The guys teased him in fun.

The groom's suit turned out very nice. Dad got some rubels again for his work. He told us he had quite a large amount together now.

He found out he would be able to buy two horses and a wagon from a farmer, a used truck, a cottage and all kinds of things.

Dad never told us how he got out of the camp. He just said I have given a promise and I will never break that promise. We figured that he had given the big amount of money to one of the truck drivers and he would have dropped dad off on a place where he could get connections to train or other transportation to go toward Germany.

The Boycott of the Jews – April 1933

The Boycott of the Jews took place before I was born, and I learned about it from family and friends as I got older. We never learned in school about all the atrocities that went on. Only parents and grandparents told all of the horror stories afterwards–when Hitler was dead.

Germany had many unemployed people. Hunger was in almost every household. That made it easier for people to believe the stories they were told. The Jews had to be sent home to their own land (Israel). We, the Germans, would have their jobs, because without the Jews there would be more [jobs] for the German people. The neediness was so great that people really believed Hitler was right. He opened factories and hired thousands of people. War materials were constructed in those factories.

Jewish doctors, professors, teachers, attorneys, judges and rabbis lost their place of work and made room for unemployed Germans. Merchants lost their stores with all the inventory. Banks were taken away from Jewish bankers. At this time, it was still possible for Jews to flee. Whoever had money or jewelry could arrange to disappear and flee to another land. The borders were not closed yet for Jews. Many went to Africa, Russia, Poland, France and Spain and lived on the money they had saved from the Germans. Some had to get jobs to survive, but had trouble with their German names; they had to change their names to be able to be employed. In Germany, synagogues were closed, so they lost their place of prayer. Jews were put into ghettos now, separated from Germans. Walls were built to keep them out of German quarters. In Obersohlesien (part of the German Reich) the Jews were undercover from the Geneva Safety Law. Germans called it the Minderheitsabkommen. Jews could not be harassed there and could live in peace until April 1st, 1935, when the Safety Law expired.

The Mob (Nazis) painted David Stars on windows and doors of Jewish homes, stores and banks occupied by Jews. The Mob created violence, smashed windows, broke down doors and stole everything they could from the Jewish people. Years later I could see David Stars on walls and houses with my own eyes.

In 1939, Great Britain declared war with Germany. Berlin and Dresden were bombs, air raids came every day until almost no homes were standing anymore. In Poland, Warsaw was destroyed by bombs. Thousands and thousands of people walked away without knowing where to go to. They were just trying to get away from the Nazis. But the German army marched through the streets of Berlin, their boots clicking on the cobblestones, singing happy marching songs ("Auf der Heide blueht ein Kleines Bluemelein, und dass heist Erika"). And Hitler spoke every day over the speaker, "We will win this war. Heil Hitler!"

Glass-Night was the night when all the windows of Jewish homes and stores were broken by the Mob and Nazis on Nov. 9, 1939. Fires were set, stones and Molotov cocktails were thrown into houses and stores. There were no police helping the Jews; they just let the violence happen. It went on for a long time.

Jewish men, women, and children were loaded up in trucks, being pushed and shoved by bayonets and gun butts. They were transported to the train stations and loaded into cattle trains. Some of the trains had no roofs, so if it would rain or snow, the poor creatures had to endure it. Most transports went to Auschwitz and other concentration camps in Germany. Later on they went to Poland and many other places. There were no toilets on the cattle trains. Nobody was allowed to get off the train, and a bucket was put into every compartment which would be emptied when the train stopped somewhere. It must have been so humiliating. Sometimes there were so many people in one car; they had to stand up body to body.

* * *

Around 1940, immigration was still possible if you had gold, money, silver, paintings, jewelry or connections. Not so lucky were the ones staying in Germany, Poland, and the East Block. Transport after transport of children, women and men would be hauled away. Families were ripped apart. Whoever did stop or could not walk fast enough was shot on the spot.

A long time later, we found out what really happened. Old people and sick people, little girls and boys, would be loaded on trucks, and the whole transport went to the cemetery after going through the gas chambers. We were told that 6 million Jewish people had lost their lives–what a shame. The ones in the camps had to live on water soup, and now and then, an old piece of bread, and they had to work until they passed out. Many had to help the Gestapo to burn their own people. Children, grandparents, pregnant women, relatives, brothers, uncles or aunts; it was all a must, and if you refused to go, you got shot.

It was so amazing when the survivors told us that there was no protesting. Like sheep, they walked one after the other into the showers. They called it the slaughterhouse, and they knew there was no coming back. Proud and with dignity, they went into the gas chambers. What a Volk. Why had God let it happen?

Most of the information I have is from Christa, who worked in our household. She came directly from Auschwitz to us. We, the children, were astounded over the number tattooed into her arm. We listened with amazement to the stories she told us every evening after she was done working. First she was in Buchenwald, but after she lost so much weight and got sick, they shipped her to Auschwitz where she was waiting for the day to go to the slaughterhouse herself. She was rescued by the American Army. When Dad and Mom picked her up from the train station, she still had the typical haircut of the camp people. Our parents took her in as a daughter, and we children had to promise not to be difficult to Christa. After many months in our house, her hair grew nice and long, and Mom went with her to Aunt Hilde's salon and got her a nice perm. She had to color her hair already–she was only 18 years old–but with the pain and suffering in the camps, she got all gray. We really loved her, and she stayed with us until she got married to a friend of our Dad. Schleiz 1949.

Funny Episodes

My Grandma's parents lived in a little village, and they owned a cattle farm. People in the 1800s did not get very much of an education in those days–epecially when they had to go to a one classroom schoolhouse. Great Grandpa was very shy about putting his signature on any document. One day he got too old to care for his farm himself and wanted to sign it over to his son. He locked himself in his room, drew the curtains, put a light on and tried out his signature on an old piece of paper before he put in on the document. Triumphant, he opened the door after one hour and showed off his nice signature. "God pieb Luft" said the signature, but his name was Godlieb Luft. The attorney smiled and put the document in his pack and left. Grandma went outside with him and asked if everything was ok. The attorney laughed and said he misspelled his first name, but I shouldn't give him another hour for tryouts.

Erna in Switzerland (Mom's Sister)
We had an Aunt that lived with her family in Basel, and we visited them in 1953. They had a shed in the back yard and about 20 hens. As the

grown-ups talked and talked, it got boring for the young ones, and they needed to get out of the house to get rid of their energy. So they played ball in the yard, climbed the apple tree and then somehow got into the chicken coop. Our Aunt came running because the hens were making lots of noise. She got the kids out of the coop and they had to promise not to open up that door again. After a while the children started itching, and the two little ones cried very hard. Mom checked to see what was going on and found chicken fleas all over them. They all got a very short haircut and a hot bath before they could go to bed. What an adventure.

Tante Erna (Aunt Erna)

On the same visit, our Aunt had something happen to her. She wanted to go in the basement to get a glass jar of canned peaches for after dinner. She wanted me to carry it upstairs, but the glass jar slipped out of her hands as she was giving it to me, and it crashed to the floor. What a mess. The juice was so slimy; she just slipped to the floor and did the splits. I started laughing so hard, and she tried and tried to get up, but every time she ended up doing another split. Mom came running down the stairs, stopped wisely on the last step, and rescued our poor Aunt Erna out of her splits by reaching far over with her hand, which was grabbed by Aunt Erna, and she held on for her life. I felt so sorry that I could not help her but I just could not stop laughing. Many years later, when I thought of this scene, I still had to laugh–what a picture of an older lady doing an elegant split.

Our Father

Our Father had a motorbike with a sidecar for Mom so they could go away now and then. On one nice Saturday, Papa cleaned the bike to get it ready for a little trip with Mom in the side car. They were all ready with leather helmets and white scarves, and Papa hit the pedal. He drove off, but Mom was still sitting in full gear in front of the house. He came back after a few minutes, and we laughed so hard. He took it with a good big smile.

One day, Dad came home with a new kind of heater. It looked like a lamp, but instead of a light bulb there were spirals. When he plugged in the cord, the spirals got hot and red. He always warned us to be careful while using the heater. One day he washed his car, and he had left the back window open, and the seats got wet. He put the heating lamp on the back seat and plugged it in to dry the water damage. After a while, the whole car was on fire.

Visit in the Camp

Grandma (Oma) Walli was 65 when she learned how to ride a bicycle. After two weeks, she was so bored out of her mind that she just had to do something. In the camp, there were no stores or any other social events, so she made up her mind to go to Nurnberg where all the stores, movies and theaters were. Nurnberg was 45 km away from our Camp Raitersaich by train.

Grandma Walli

Walli Oma, as we called her, came to visit with us in the refugee camp in Raitersaich. This is where we ended up for 6 long years after fleeing the Russian sector of Germany. She still lived in Berlin, and all senior citizens were able to cross the Soviet border legally. She was in her sixties or early seventies at that time. Coming out of a big city, she was not used to having any stores around for miles. She was used to going window shopping and buying whatever she needed, any time she needed to. We were out of the city 60 miles, and Nurnberg was the next biggest city. Our sister, Evie, heard her complaining that she missed the stores so much, that she told her she could take our bike. Grandma could not ride a bike. She had a disability with her hip so she could not walk very far either. Evie knew the answer to everything, so she told Grandma to learn to ride the bike, and I will teach you, she said.

Walli Oma (Grandma)

Dad's Mom, Walli, went with our sister, Evie, out to the field ways to help Grandma learn to ride a bicycle. After a while, Grandma was very good with the bike. One morning, she took the bike and yelled over her shoulder to Mom, "I am going to Nurnberg, be back later." Mom was shocked that Grandma was going to Nurnberg by bike. 60 miles on this old bike? But Evie told her that Grandma will only go to the railroad station and then take the train. Mom just shook her head. Grandma came home in the evening all happy, but very tired.

We could not go and visit our Grandma in East Germany after deserting the Soviet Sector. We were on the Black list and banned to enter again.

Dad

The only bible verse our Dad was ever to quote was: "Da komt eine lange durre." This has a double meaning and is funny in the German language. The English translation is "there is a drought coming," but drought in German means a skinny, tall, slim person. Our Grandparents and Mom were very religious, and that's how Dad showed his humor and that he read the Bible, too. Franz Otto, our Uncle, Hildegard's husband, was often called that quote by Dad "tall and skinny is coming."

Berlin Grandma Walli

She had a little bit of a temper every so often. Her husband, our Grandpa, liked to go for a beer or two when he went shopping. One time, Grandma ran out of butter in the morning. She was hungry and asked Opa, as we called him, to go to the store and get a pound of butter. Grandpa went, but had to stop for a beer. His coworkers were waiting for a third person to play a game of cards (Skat). Grandpa thought one game would be ok. It was late afternoon when he finally got out, because he had a winning streak and ended up with quite a bit of money. The butter got a little soft in the meantime. As he came into the house, Grandma yelled at him. She grabbed the butter, and as she felt it being so soft, in her anger, she threw it on the wall. For years to come, after every coat of paint, the spot came right through, as the paint dried. This is a story that keeps us still grinning, thinking of Walli Oma.

Elastic Was Not As It Is Today

Every Sunday, my husband gave me a few hours to myself. He went to the movies with the children and visited with his parents. I walked proudly, feeling good on the Main promenade where all the expensive stores were. The store windows mirrored my reflection. Not bad, I thought to myself, I looked pretty good. There were many folks out window shopping that day. Suddenly I felt something silky slipping down my legs. Oh my God, the elastic in my underwear had ripped, and my underwear had fallen off. Elegantly, I stepped out of them. I bent down and picked them up, scrunching them in my purse. I looked to see if anyone had noticed and went on walking as if nothing had happened. My family still laughs about that one.

My memories and true stories ...

Helga Kelly now lives in Wausaukee, Wisconsin.